# WOMEN OF FAITH™
## STUDY GUIDE SERIES

# A LIFE OF
# WORSHIP

## FOREWORD BY

# SHEILA
# WALSH

## THOMAS NELS
### Since 1798

NASHVILLE   DALLAS   MEXICO CITY   RIO DE JANEIRO

D1417730

Published by Thomas Nelson, Inc.
P.O. Box 141000, Nashville, Tennessee, 37214.

Thomas Nelson, Inc. titles may be purchased in bulk for educational, business, fund-raising, or sales promotional use. For information, please e-mail SpecialMarkets@ThomasNelson.com.

ISBN-13: 978-0-7852-5154-5

10 WC 16

# ✦ CONTENTS ✦

# ✦ FOREWORD ✦

When my son, Christian, turned seven in December of 2004, Barry and I bought him a puppy. The first time he held this fluffy little Bichon Frise I could tell he had fallen in love. He named her Belle. I watched how they interacted for the first few days, not wanting his boyish enthusiasm to scare her and overshadow his loving, tender heart. They learned each other's ways, and within a week she slept at the end of his bed at night. When I asked him what it felt like to have his own puppy, he replied with passion, "Mom, I was made for this!"

I believe in a profound, spiritual way we all long for that sense of purpose. We want to know what we were made for. We want to know that our life matters and we are living it as well as we can. Perhaps, like me, you often fall into bed at night amazed that another day is over, and it seems as if all you have managed to do is corral the daily chaos in your home. The laundry is done again! Food has been cooked, consumed, and cleared up one more time. You didn't fit in the twenty minutes of exercise you had hoped to do or read more than a few lines of the book on your bedside table. Those are things that only you will notice if they are missed. The other list affects our families, and skipping them is not an option. We want to be good wives, good mothers, and trusted friends. But these things do not, in themselves, fulfill our passionate longing to know what we were made for.

I have found the answer, the glorious treasure, in a life of worship.

I don't know what comes to your mind when you reflect on a life of worship. Perhaps you think of the fifteen minutes or two hours, depending on your denomination, that you spend on your feet on a Sunday morning in church. You may

# ✦ INTRODUCTION ✦

*I know few people who take adequate time for reflection—and many who regret that they don't. Who said, "The important always gets sacrificed on the altar of the urgent?" Taking time is a better way to live. Let's reflect on who we are, where we're going, and the life God has given us.*

## —Luci Swindoll

Let me put a question before you: Whose job is it to glorify God? Of all of the things God created, what beings were especially designed to give God glory and praise and honor? The image that leaps immediately to mind involves radiant light, white robes and halos, beating wings, and uplifted voices—"Holy, holy, holy." Cherubim and seraphim surround the Father's throne, worshiping and praising. They give God glory 24/7, and they will for all eternity. When it comes to giving proper honor to God, the angels are perfectly suited to their task.

But wait! Are the angels the only ones created to give glory to God? Of course not. So were we. God especially designed us to bring glory and honor and praise to Him too. Now most of us wouldn't want to be the act following the angel chorus. Can you imagine? After all that majestic beauty and pure light, we'd look pretty small and dim. Alone on the stage, we feel insignificant in our abilities, feeble in our efforts, and unsure of our next move. But we needn't fear. Angels just do what angels are meant to do. We shouldn't try to be angels. We are asked to be women who do what women were made to do. And when our lives glorify our Heavenly Father, we captivate our audiences. Even the angels stand in amazement.

think of the CDs you play in the house as you attack the daily chores. Those are part of my life too, but they are not what I mean by a life of worship. Jesus lived a life of worship. He lived every moment of every day with a "Yes!" in His spirit to His Father. His declared intent was solely to do the will of His Father. Jesus worshipped as He healed the blind and the lame. He worshipped as He cleansed the temple, driving from its holy halls those who would turn it into a Wal-Mart for worshippers. He worshipped in the Garden of Gethsemane as He prayed that the cup of the wrath of God might pass from Him. He worshipped on Calvary's brutal tree of death. In every way, at every moment, Jesus lived a life of worship.

If you long to know what you were made for, you can find that peace and purpose in a life of worship. There is no more liberating way to live than to wake up every day with a "Yes!" to God. Worshipping in all the moments of our lives changes us because we move from trying to be perfect to resting in the perfect will of a God who loves us passionately.

I pray that as you travel through this book you will be able to say with my son, "I was made for this!"

*—Sheila Walsh*

We are not able to wing our way into heaven and add our voices to the celestial choir. We can't be expected to set aside our responsibilities and spend all day in worship—can we? In this study, we are going to take a careful look at how we can glorify God in our everyday lives.

*Whoever offers praise glorifies Me;*
*And to him who orders his conduct aright*
*I will show the salvation of God.*

**Psalm 50:23**

# CHAPTER 1

# DEFINING GLORY

## "BUT TRULY, AS I LIVE, ALL THE EARTH SHALL BE FILLED WITH THE GLORY OF THE LORD."

### Numbers 14:21

Glory is a common word in the Christian vocabulary, but how do you define it? We talk about God's glory: "Thine is the power and the glory forever." We sing about God's glory: "To God be the glory, great things He has done." We want to give God glory: "Glory to God in the highest." But what does it mean to glorify something?

The dictionary defines glory as great honor, praise, admiration, distinction, fame, and renown. To glorify something is to praise or honor it, acknowledge its excellence, give it homage, exalt, and worship it. In other words, we glorify God when we tell Him how much we admire Him, when we give Him proper honor, and when we acknowledge His perfection and power. We can pray it, we can say it, we can sing it, and we can

## CLEARING ✦ THE ✦ COBWEBS

All parts of God's creation, great or small, bring glory to God. Which ones are your favorites?

proclaim it to others. Glorifying God draws attention to His character, lifts up His mighty deeds for others to see, and focuses our attention on Him. This act of praise highlights, emphasizes, magnifies, worships, and adores.

**1.** David wrote many psalms urging his people to give God glory. He assigned Asaph and the other Levites to perform a beautiful psalm when the Ark was brought into the holy city. Why does 1 Chronicles 16:29 say we should give the LORD glory?

**2.** So often we think of God receiving glory. Did you know God also gives glory? Look up the following Scripture texts and match them to the thing God has glorified.

|  |  |
|---|---|
| \_\_\_ Exodus 29:43 | a. God glorifies own name. |
| \_\_\_ Isaiah 60:7 | b. God glorifies His Son. |
| \_\_\_ Jeremiah 30:19 | c. God glorifies His Temple. |
| \_\_\_ John 12:28 | d. God glorifies His tabernacle. |
| \_\_\_ John 13:31 | e. God glorifies His people. |

**3.** Parents give glory to their children when they tell them how proud they are of them. God modeled this for us. He didn't hold back in giving glory to His Son. How does Peter recall God's praise of Jesus in 2 Peter 1:17?

**4.** In the Book of Hebrews, the writer explores the amazing place Jesus holds in God's plan for our salvation. How is Jesus described in Hebrews 1:3?

> *How does one find God? He is in our prayers guiding our words, He is in our songs as we worship Him, and He is filling our mouths when we comfort a friend or speak wisdom to someone who needs hope. Count your blessings. He is in them too.*
>
> Patsy Clairmont

*H*ave you ever eaten glorified rice? It's a kind of salad made from leftover rice. You combine the cold rice with bits of pineapple and oranges, marshmallows, and whipped cream. The resulting dish is still rice, but it has been transformed— glorified! We do the same thing at Christmas time. We roam the slopes of a tree farm and examine the different pine trees. At a distance, they all look the same, but once we have chosen one and set it apart from the others, we glorify it. We adorn it with bright, beautiful things, embellishing its branches until it shines. An ordinary woman can be glorified in many ways. One way is when she becomes a bride. Set apart from every other woman, she is adorned, jeweled, and veiled. She glows with the joy of her wedding day.

When God glorifies something, He starts with something quite ordinary. A place is just like any other place unless God's presence makes it holy. A woman is just like any other woman until God's presence marks her as His own. Though we are ordinary, we have been chosen. Though we are common, we have been touched by the divine. Though we were just like everyone else, we are now robed in righteousness, veiled in holiness, and adorned with spiritual gifts. God glorifies us.

**5.** Does God glorify something just so that it will be glorified? No. There is always a very good reason why God does what He does. Why does Jesus say God has glorified Him in John 17:1?

*"In this you greatly rejoice, though now for a little while you may have had to suffer grief in all kinds of trials." These trials have come, the Scripture says, "so that your faith—of greater worth than gold, which perishes even though refined by fire—may be proved genuine" (1 Peter 1:6, 7). This genuine, refined by fire, holding–on–for–dear–life faith will result in praise and glory to Christ.*

Nicole Johnson

**6.** There are a few more things we can learn about giving glory and receiving glory. In the first place, we must consider the proper source of glory. What does Hebrews 5:5 say Jesus did *not* do?

**7.** God gives the glory, and He gives it to those He has made. What does Psalm 8:4–6 say about the glory God has given to mankind?

**8.** What does God give to us, according to Psalm 84:11?

*It is easy to believe that God can use our lives when we see immediate results, when positive feedback encourages us to push on. It is hard to keep walking when we see little sign that what we are doing is making a difference.*

Sheila Walsh

**9.** God deserves glory. God gives glory. Where is your glory, according to Psalm 62:7?

## ✦ DIGGING DEEPER ✦

The ordinary becomes extraordinary when it is touched by God. Take a look at these passages. What happens in each verse when the LORD touches someone?

- Isaiah 6:7
- Matthew 8:15
- Luke 7:14
- Jeremiah 1:9
- Mark 1:41

## ✦ PONDER & PRAY ✦

Over the next several days, open your eyes to the things that bring glory to God: His creation, His people, His plan, His Word, His Son, and His Spirit. What can you do to contribute to God's glory? This week, your prayer can be for God to touch your own life. Pray that your life will bring glory to God's name.

## ✦ TRINKETS TO TREASURE ✦

At the close of every Women of Faith conference, women are asked to play a little game of pretend. Each conference guest is asked to imagine a gift has been placed in her hands—one from each of the speakers—to serve as reminders of the different lessons shared. This study guide will carry on this tradition! At the close of each lesson, you will be presented with a small gift. Though imaginary, it will serve to remind you of the things you have learned. Think of it as a souvenir. Souvenirs are little trinkets we pick up on our journeys to remind us of where we have been. They keep us from forgetting the path we have traveled. Hide these little treasures in your heart, for as you ponder on them, they will draw you closer to God.

## ✦ TRINKETS TO TREASURE ✦

Your trinket for this first week will remind you that all glory belongs to God. He is worthy of glory, and glory is His to give. Your gift is a small handful of rice. Bland and humble and common enough—until it is glorified. Just remember when God glorifies something, it is so the glory can be returned to Him. Live a life that brings glory to God!

## ✦ NOTES & PRAYER REQUESTS ✦

# ✦ Notes & Prayer Requests ✦

# CHAPTER 2

# ONE WORTHY

## "FOR MY OWN SAKE, FOR MY OWN SAKE, I WILL DO IT; FOR HOW SHOULD MY NAME BE PROFANED? AND I WILL NOT GIVE MY GLORY TO ANOTHER."

### Isaiah 48:11

Being number one is very important in our world. The media keeps us posted on which movies are blockbusters, which books are best–sellers, which songs are the most popular, and which television programs are award–winning. We crown homecoming queens, judge beauty pageants, and host talent competitions. There are Super Bowls and World Series games and Olympics. We watch the numbers, charting the rise and fall percentage points, stock prices, front–runners, team standings, record sales, profit margins, and bottom lines. People claw their way to the summit. It's like a grown–up version of King of the Hill. And those who make it to

## CLEARING ✦ THE ✦ COBWEBS

It's said that everyone receives their fifteen minutes of fame in this life. Have you had yours yet?

> *God's desire is that His Word and His Spirit be guides for life. Being a follower of Jesus Christ means becoming more and more like Him—letting His spirit transform us into all we were created to be. That happens, dear friends, from the inside out.*
>
> Luci Swindoll

the top achieve fame and fortune—for as long as they can defend their title.

It is easy to get caught up in this search for significance. We all want to accomplish something in our lives and be recognized for it. But in doing so, we are trying to gain glory for ourselves. The Bible reminds us that, in the end, there is only One who is worthy of glory. No matter what the polls and charts and nominations might be, in the end, all the glory belongs to God.

**1.** There is one worthy of all glory—God. Look up these Scriptures that give us some of His more glorious names.

- Psalm 24:10 became the text for one of the songs in Handel's Messiah. What it ascribe to God?
- How does Paul describe God in Ephesians 1:17?
- How is Jesus named in both 1 Corinthians 2:8 and James 2:1?

**2.** What is the psalmist's prayer in Psalm 115:1? Can you echo it?

**3.** God is a jealous God and does not share His glory with any other. He wrote it right into the Ten Commandments (It's number two, actually.) What does God say about His glory in Isaiah 42:8?

**4.** God is one–of–a–kind and uniquely worthy of honor. What He has done, none can attempt. What He is, none can hope to be. According to the heavenly chorus in Revelation 4:11, why does the LORD deserve glory?

**5.** Let's make a list. What does Revelation 5:12 say Jesus is worthy to receive?

*We will go through trials, but we can submit to them so that our faith, the most precious thing we have, may be authentic. When people see our lives they know we are honest people. Suffering makes us real, and that brings glory to God.*

Nicole Johnson

*T*here is a game my three–year old loves to play. It comes up in all kinds of moments—during bath time, car rides, and while I'm tucking him in for his nap. It's a simple game, but it's one he loves. "Who's the biggest?" he'll ask loudly. "Who's the biggest and the strongest?" My job is then to offer suggestions. I'll wrack my brains for creative answers—ones that will make him laugh. But no matter what solutions I offer to his query, his smiling answer is always "No!"

"Is it Daddy? Is it Grandpa? Is it a whale? Is it a truck? Is it a bear? Is it a mountain?" Finally, when I give up guessing, he'll proudly announce the answer he thinks I didn't know. "Jesus!" To my little guy, Jesus is the biggest and the strongest and the fastest and the best. Jesus is his hero, the One worthy of admiration. He's my hero, too.

> LORD, *how frequently and mindlessly we kick against the very constraints you put in place for our growth and refinement. Remind those of us who get so caught up with the earthly that to do so is to miss the heavenly. Your plan for each of us is not one of earthly ease but of heavenly peace. Amen.*
>
> Marilyn Meberg

6. Where is God's glory visible to us? Psalm 97:6 tells us one place where His glory is on display.

**7.** For some, the glories of creation are not enough. What did Moses ask of God in Exodus 33:18?

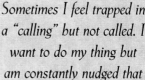

**8.** Later, when the Tabernacle and the Temple had been constructed, the people were awed by the visible indication of God's presence in their midst—the Shekinah Glory. What do Psalm 26:8 and Psalm 63:2 say about God's glory?

> *Sometimes I feel trapped in a "calling" but not called. I want to do my thing but am constantly nudged that God wants me to do His thing. I feel resentful toward God for that. I don't like the feeling.*
>
> Luci Swindoll

**9.** What should our reaction be to the LORD's glorious presence in our hearts and lives? Perhaps it should compare to the response of God's people to Him in 2 Chronicles 7:3.

**10.** God alone is worthy of such honor and praise. Even the Old Testament prophets knew God would be glorified. What does Habakkuk 2:14 say about God's glory?

## ✦ DIGGING DEEPER ✦

The Scriptures say God alone is worthy of praise. Even His name is worthy of honor and respect. Take a look at these Scripture passages. They each speak of the glorious name of God.

- Psalm 8:1
- Psalm 29:2
- Psalm 72:19
- Psalm 105:3
- Psalm 148:13

## ✦ PONDER & PRAY ✦

"I will praise the LORD according to His righteousness, And will sing praise to the name of the LORD Most High" (Ps. 7:17). We praise God, giving Him glory, because of who He is. When finding ways and reasons to give God glory, His character is a good place to start. As you ponder and pray this week, search for the reasons why God is worthy of praise. Ask yourself, "Why is He the only One worthy?" Then make your list the basis of your times of devotion and worship.

## ✦ TRINKETS TO TREASURE ✦

People put value on things that are rare—hard to find or one of a kind. That's why gold is a precious metal. That's why diamonds are so costly. That's why antiques and original pieces of art are so valuable. God has always loved rare and unique things. After all, He makes snowflakes, and no two are alike. And He made each person on this earth a one–of–a–kind masterpiece, so we are rare and precious too. But we all know that, while there are many people, there is only one God. That's why we sing, "LORD, You are more precious than silver. LORD, You are more costly than gold." So this week's treasure will be a gold coin, to remind you of how God is more precious than the most costly things on earth. He is one and only, and therefore worthy of all glory.

## ✦ NOTES & PRAYER REQUESTS ✦

# ✦ NOTES & PRAYER REQUESTS ✦

# CHAPTER 3

# OUR VERY PURPOSE

### "I WANT THEM BACK, EVERY LAST ONE WHO BEARS MY NAME, EVERY MAN, WOMAN, AND CHILD WHOM I CREATED FOR MY GLORY, YES, PERSONALLY FORMED AND MADE EACH ONE."

**Isaiah 43:7 MSG**

Have you bought any technological gizmos lately? You know what I mean — computers, scanners, cell phones, palm–pilots, DVD players, MP3 players, stereo systems, digital cameras, microwave ovens, answering machines, juicers, food processors, bread machines, cappuccino makers. The pleasure of owning something shiny and new quickly fades in the face of troubling questions. "What does this button do?" "What is this switch for?" "How do I get it to do this?" The more these devices are designed to make life easier for us, the more complicated the instructions are for using them. I took pride in knowing how to set the time on our old VCR. Now I can't decipher what all those buttons on a television remote

## CLEARING + THE + COBWEBS

Most people equate their purpose in life with the roles they currently hold. What are some of the roles you are holding right now — mother, caregiver, committee chair, grandmother, teacher, supervisor, peacemaker, administrator, wife?

are for. Who *uses* all those buttons anyway? If you're really going to get the most out of your new thingamajig, you have to haul out the owner's manual. With a little patience and a degree in Rocket Science, you can wade through the technical jargon, and you're on your way!

Unfortunately, life doesn't come with an owner's manual. There may not be a lot of buttons to push, but we have to decide what to plug into. There are choices and commitments to make, and there's no troubleshooting section we can turn to for help. What we wouldn't give for a mission statement, even if we had to wade through a lot of technical jargon to discover it. A juicer makes juice. A camera takes pictures. An answering machine takes messages. And a person was designed to…what?

*How do we truly give up our agendas? How do we genuinely say, "not my will but Yours, LORD"? For me, the answer to that question is found in my understanding and acceptance of God's sovereignty. All happenings on this earth and in my life are worked out in conformity with His purpose—not mine, but His.*

Marilyn Meberg

**1.** Why *did* God make people? We've turned out to be something of a bother, and yet God keeps us around! In Isaiah 43:7, why does Isaiah say we were created?

**2.** Thankfully, we are not alone in this purpose. What else gives glory to God, according to David in Psalm 19:1?

**3.** Who will bring glory to God, according to Revelation 5:13?

> *Perhaps there is little immediate satisfaction in what you have been called to do, but if you will faithfully push on through the night the LORD is the one who carries a reward in His hands.*
>
> Sheila Walsh

**4.** So is that what we find all of creation doing right now? Are we fulfilling our original purpose? If not, what went wrong? Romans 3:23 names the problem point blank.

Not only does our life come without an owner's manual, but our hardware is faulty. We have a fatal error in our systems. Sin is in the works, and it's messing up our motherboard. It's like a glitch in the programming, or a virus or a worm. It confuses us, blinds us, and woos us away from the Creator. Instead of living a life that glorifies God, we work against God and His plans. We're still living and doing things, but they're all the wrong kinds of things! It's like trying to make toast in a blender or bake cookies in the washing machine.

**5.** The people of the earth were all made to glorify God, but sin took hold, and so God had to start small. Look at the progression in these verses.

- Where did God start? Who first gave glory to God, according to Psalm 22:23?
- Who shall come and worship the LORD, according to Psalm 86:9?
- In the end, who will give glory to the Father, according to Philippians 2:11?

*What are you resisting? Has God been nudging you into action and you've either said "no" repeatedly, or "well, maybe" so weakly that no one can hear it? I can tell you from my own experience, the very thing we say "no" to just might be God's blessing in disguise. He wants to bless us; He wants to mature us; He wants to get us out of our comfort zone.*

Luci Swindoll

**6.** How does God work on us, repairing us if you will, to bring us back around to our glorious purpose? Paul offers a beautiful description in 2 Corinthians 3:18.

**7.** What else does Paul say about the way our lives should glorify God in 1 Corinthians 6:20?

**8.** What does God promise in Psalm 50:15, and what is our response?

**9.** Jude's benediction talks about both these things — God's hand in our lives and God's worthiness to be glorified. What two things does Jude say God does for us in verse 24? And what does he give in return to God in verse 25?

## ✦ DIGGING DEEPER ✦

It's very easy to begin to think, "Hey, I'm not so bad." Unfortunately, that very attitude is proof of sin's subtle hold. In order to root out the sin in our hearts, we must humble ourselves, call a spade a spade (well, a sin a sin), and take it before God in confession. Let's look at a few verses that can help us with sin and renewal.

- John 8:34
- Romans 7:15–20
- James 1:15
- Romans 6:12, 13
- Hebrews 3:13
- 1 John 1:8

## ✦ PONDER & PRAY ✦

This week, make glory your purpose and your prayer. Ask God to continue His work in remaking you so you can fulfill your original design. Pray for sharp eyes to detect the sin that gets in the way, and a soft heart willing to confess and change its ways. The changes in your spirit will stand as testimony to every person who knows you. You can join all of creation in declaring God's goodness, majesty, and love.

## ✦ TRINKETS TO TREASURE ✦

As a child, one of the first verses I learned was Psalm 19:1, "The heavens declare the glory of God." When we consider the stars, we are impressed. The vastness, the majesty, the complexity, the beauty—all point to the greatness of our God. But we, too, bring glory to God. Our one, little life can declare the glory of God as effectively as all the stars in the heavens. So your trinket this week is a star. Let it remind you not to be discouraged. The stars fulfill their purpose, and so do we. No matter how small your efforts and your effectiveness might seem, keep on twinkling, little star!

## ✦ NOTES & PRAYER REQUESTS ✦

## ✦ NOTES & PRAYER REQUESTS ✦

# CHAPTER 4

# WHAT TIME IS GOOD FOR YOU?

### "BUT THE HOUR IS COMING, AND NOW IS, WHEN TRUE WORSHIPERS WILL WORSHIP THE FATHER IN SPIRIT AND TRUTH; FOR THE FATHER IS SEEKING SUCH TO WORSHIP HIM."

**John 4:23**

So many of us had no inkling we were supposed to be living for God's glory. We didn't even know it was in the mission statement. And so we're faced with a small dilemma: "Whoops! I didn't know this was my purpose for living. Maybe I should work a little glorification into my daily routine." And so you open up your planners and flip through your calendars and try to work it in. Things are already packed in pretty tight, so finding a timeslot is going to be tricky. It's no simple matter to graft a brand–new mission statement onto a life already set in its ways. Should you re–prioritize your day, making room for God's glory? Or perhaps

## CLEARING
## ✦ THE ✦
## COBWEBS

Are you a night owl, or more of a morning person?

it would be best to keep your usual schedule, just carving out a few extra minutes in the morning. You could set the alarm. If you're not a morning person, then maybe it would be better to burn the midnight oil, giving God some night owl quality time. What do you think? When is it appropriate to glorify God?

**1.** When should we glorify the LORD, according to Isaiah 24:15?

*God speaks to us clearly. He means what He says. When He says He'll provide, we can count on that. When He promises peace, wisdom, strength, or comfort, they are ours. God imparts His word and keeps it. His words matter! I find tremendous comfort in that!*

Luci Swindoll

**2.** While Isaiah greets the dawning with praise, David proves to be an even earlier riser. His worship has begun before the sun rises. What are the first words out of his mouth in the wee hours of the morning in Psalm 57:8–11?

**3.** Those who love and fear God find reasons for rejoicing...when? Look in Psalm 65:8 for that answer.

**4.** Why limit your chances to glorify God to the day? When does David say He finds time to communicate with his LORD? He mentions his meditations in both Psalm 63:6 and Psalm 119:148.

**5.** We've covered the morning and the evening and all through the night. Guess what's left? When does the psalmist say he will give praise to God? Check Psalm 44:8 and also Psalm 89:16.

> *Dear friend, embrace your day—this day—it is a gift. Take the LORD's hand. He will help you to unwrap the day and then to celebrate it. And His grace will be sufficient for any need you have.*
>
> Patsy Clairmont

**6.** So how long will this last? What does Psalm 75:9 say to that?

**7.** Though we praise the LORD from now until our very last breath, God's glory will not cease just because we do. The Scriptures make it clear, over and over again, that God will have the glory for…how long? Read Philippians 4:20 for the answer.

*R*emember Esther? She was faced with a difficult choice. Should she risk her life for the sake of her people? Or should she just keep quiet and hope everything would blow over? Even as she was contemplating her options, her wise cousin Mordecai sent her a stunning message: "Just because you live in the king's palace, don't think that out of all the Jewish people you alone will escape. If you keep quiet at this time, someone else will help and save the Jewish people, but you and your father's family will all die" (Esth. 4:13, 14 NCV). Esther might have refused to stand up for her people, but if she had refused, that would not have sealed their fate. God would just use someone else to fulfill His purposes.

In the same way, we have a choice. We can glorify God in our lives and reap eternal benefits for our pains. Or we can try to hide from God's purposes and ignore our LORD's calling. But if we do that, we may very well be passed over, and our place given to another. We might miss out on something truly amazing. God *will* be glorified, with or without our help. Wouldn't you rather be a part of that?

> *Sometimes we know we need refreshment but are too lazy in the routine of life—or too preoccupied with what we think is "important"—to stop for spiritual replenishment. Sometimes life may crowd in on us enough that we are simply not aware of our need.*
>
> Sheila Walsh

**8.** God can use anything for His glory, even the most unlikely people. Remember reluctant Jonah? Sly Jacob? Busy Martha? Take a look at Romans 9:17. Whom did God raise up and for what purpose?

> *The Creator has made us each one of a kind. There is nobody else exactly like us, and there never will be. Each of us is His special creation and is alive for a distinctive purpose. Because of this, the person we are, and the contribution we make by being that very person, are vitally important to God.*
>
> Luci Swindoll

**9.** So, if you are going to "Praise the LORD! Praise God in His Sanctuary; Praise Him in His mighty firmament!" (Ps. 150:1), when's a good time for you?

## ✦ DIGGING DEEPER ✦

There is something poetic about the different doxologies and benedictions we find throughout the Bible. Some of their phrases have become so familiar they roll off our tongues with a triumphant ring. We love them because they so eloquently sum up the truth. Look at these verses. Each takes up the familiar strain that God will be glorified forever.

- Psalm 104:31
- Galatians 1:5
- 1 Peter 5:11
- Romans 11:36
- Ephesians 3:21

## ✦ PONDER & PRAY ✦

This week, let your prayer be "Yes, LORD!" Tell Him you want to answer His calling. Tell Him you want to be a part of His plans. Instead of trying to fit God's glory into your comfortable routines, ask God to show you how to rearrange your life so it fits around *His* central purposes. Everyone will be forced to give God the glory eventually, but let Him know you want to bring Him glory right now—and from now on.

## ✦ TRINKETS TO TREASURE ✦

Did you realize when we give God our lives, we are really telling Him we want Him to have all our years, our months, and our days? Now, your mornings and your evenings belong to Him. Every hour should be lived for His glory. Every precious moment belongs to our LORD. Quite a commitment, isn't it? This week's small gift is a clock. As it marks the hours and minutes of your day, let it remind you to fill those time slots with the things that bring glory to your Heavenly Father. When you are living for Him, you can make every second count!

## ✦Notes & Prayer Requests✦

## ✦ NOTES & PRAYER REQUESTS ✦

# CHAPTER 5

# ON A GRAND SCALE

### "BY THIS MY FATHER IS GLORIFIED, THAT YOU BEAR MUCH FRUIT, SO YOU WILL BE MY DISCIPLES."

**John 15:8**

*I*n my early teens, I discovered the world of cross–stitch embroidery. I had watched my Aunt Diane stitching up a Santa Claus pattern for Christmas during one of our fall get–togethers, and she gave me a scrap of fabric and some thread. Also, my Aunt Mary Jean had huge stacks of books with patterns in them, which she said I could borrow. I was soon spending all of my allowance on cross–stitch patterns, aida fabric, and embroidery floss. The only problem was, I didn't really want to start at the beginning. The easy projects were for jar lids or bookmarks. Boring! I wanted to do something I could frame and hang on the wall. The same thing happened when I started quilting. Anybody could do a nine–patch or trip–around–the–world quilt. I started

## CLEARING
### ✦ THE ✦
## COBWEBS

Since the Tower of Babel, people have had a hankering to do things on a grand scale. The Statue of Liberty, Mount Rushmore, the Oscar Mayer® Weinermobile, and even the world's largest ball of twine. What kinds of "grand scale" attractions have you seen?

with Dresden® plates and then tackled a double wedding ring quilt. Something inside of me was impatient. I didn't want to waste time doing anything that was just a stepping–stone for the next thing. I wanted to leap ahead to where I knew I wanted to be in the end. Taking things one step at a time is difficult for me. I'd rather do things on a grand scale.

I think some of us face the same quandary in our spiritual lives. We want to glorify God in our lives, and we think that means we have to do something really big, really grand, and really impressive. So we do one of two things: either we rush ahead and try to do too much all at once, or else we hang back because we don't think we're good enough to do something great for God. Which one of these camps are you in?

**1.** How many of you have faced your spiritual life and thought to yourself, *I wish I could be like David. I'd love to be known as a woman after God's own heart!* Would you also like to tackle David's spiritual goal? What does he promise to do in Psalm 45:17?

*Why do I sometimes get bogged down with chores, hating the day? Then, at other times, I get fired up with enthusiasm, loving the day? Perspective! Perspective is everything.*

Luci Swindoll

**2.** God calls many, but He calls us all to different things. God called David to reach whole generations of people with the story of his life and with his songs. You might not be able to do that, but is there something you can do to affect just one generation—say, the next generation? What does Deuteronomy 4:9 say we can do?

**3.** God is glorified through things we many not even be considering. We don't need to found an orphanage or start a radio ministry in order to reflect God's glory. What amazing thing does Peter say we are able to do, according to 1 Peter 1:8, 9?

**4.** Take a look at Psalm 21:4–6. What, according to verse 5, has brought glory into David's life—a glory which he now returns to the LORD in writing this psalm?

> Sometimes we search so hard for the miraculous that we miss the obvious reality of His ever–present nearness.
>
> Patsy Clairmont

**5.** We want to do big things for God too, but is that what God is asking us to do? For some of us, the answer might be yes. But for some of us, our daydreams and ambitions are getting in the way of the things right in front of us. God honors those who choose to be faithful, even in the smallest of things. How does Luke put it in Luke 16:10?

*Y*ears ago, I read a wonderful illustration about spiritual fruit, and it has always remained with me. Let's say our lives are like those of apple trees. In the natural growth process, a tree buds and blooms and apples come in their season. Too often we are in a hurry to see results in our spiritual lives. We want to be wise *now*. We want to be mature *now*. We want to be respected, admired, and sought after. And so, in our hurry, we begin to tie already ripened apples onto the branches of our spiritual trees. These borrowed apples look wonderful on the trees—for a while. But their glory passes quickly because they have no connection to the tree. There is nothing to sustain them, so they get spoiled where they hang. True spiritual fruit grows over time. You can't rush it, and you can't sham it. So don't think you can bring God glory more impressively by pretending to be someone you aren't. The Tree knows the truth about who and what we really are.

**6.** You belong to Jesus, which gives you a unique opportunity, no matter what your life holds. What does Paul say will happen, according to 2 Thessalonians 1:12?

**7.** With this in mind, how then should we act? Jesus gives us His own wise course in Matthew 5:16. What does He ask of us?

**8.** Paul calls it walking worthy of our calling. What course does he recommend in Romans 2:7?

**9.** Finally, lets take a look at Peter's sage advice. What does he urge us to do in 1 Peter 4:11, and what will be the result of it?

*Your idea of creating a place to be with yourself may not be the same as mine, and that's fine. But I can promise you that until you learn that solitude is your friend and not your enemy, until you are comfortable "staying in your own orbit," you will have little to give anyone else.*

Luci Swindoll

## ✦ DIGGING DEEPER ✦

We say we believe the Bible is true, yet so often we don't live in ways that reflect the teachings found there. We aren't walking the talk we're talking! This was a point Paul made throughout his epistles. He wanted those men and women who were called by the name of Christ—Christians—to live a life worthy of the name they bore. Here are just a few passages that talk about walking worthy:

- Ephesians 4:1
- 1 Thessalonians 2:12
- Colossians 1:10
- Revelation 3:4

## ✦ Ponder & Pray ✦

Oh, to be a giant in the faith! Oh, to be recognized as a prayer warrior, a saint, a woman of faith! Oh, to be able to serve the LORD on a grand scale! Let God teach you how to be faithful in small ways, and to be patient as He nurtures us along towards maturity. As you spend time with the LORD this week, pray for His help as you give Him your moments. It's easier to spend our days selfishly, for our own pleasure and convenience. It's not easy to live for someone else, but that's just what Christ has called us to do.

## ✦ Trinkets to Treasure ✦

We all want to do big things for God, but He reminds us to do first things first. Before we are asked to be faithful in big things, we must show we can be faithful in small things. This week's trinket is an apple. We may wish our life was laden with ripened spiritual fruit, but it takes time for those apples to reach maturity. Let your apple remind you to be patient as God helps you grow. Don't be tempted to tie false apples on your branches, pretending to be something you're not. Use the gifts God has given you faithfully, and your life will bring glory to God.

## ✦ Notes & Prayer Requests ✦

## ✦ NOTES & PRAYER REQUESTS ✦

# CHAPTER 6

# ONE RIGHT WAY?

"I WILL PRAISE YOU, O LORD MY GOD, WITH ALL MY
HEART, AND I WILL GLORIFY YOUR NAME
FOREVERMORE."

**Psalm 86:12**

*I* like to do things my own way. Because of this, I don't like to ask for help with things. I think other people do things all wrong. Well, okay, not wrong maybe—but different from how I like things to be! It's not that I don't appreciate help, but I just have to do it over to suit my liking once they're done. Don't we all have certain things that we like a certain way? Some may be fussy about the protocol of business meetings, the precision of accounting spreadsheets, or the arrangement of icons on their computer desktop. While others are fussy about how the dishwasher gets loaded, how the glasses are lined up in the cupboards, which direction the stripes on the couch pillows go, how the washcloths, dishtowels, and underwear get

## CLEARING
## ✦ THE ✦
## COBWEBS

We are all fussy about certain things—how our kitchen cupboards are organized, how we label and organize our filing system at work, or what brand of peanut butter we buy. What are you fussy about?

folded, how socks should be balled together, and how the pillows get stacked onto the bed. Some of my own habits have been handed down. For instance, I fold my bath towels the way my Mom does. Some of my other habits have evolved because of their efficiency, like my system for cleaning up the kitchen after meals. I sweep the floor a certain way, I vacuum a room a certain way, I iron shirts a certain way—and I like it that way.

It is very important to realize, however, that my way of stacking dishes on the drain board is not really the *right* way. It's just *my* way. So when my mother–in–law does the dishes for me, and she stacks the dishes her way, it's not the wrong way. God made us each uniquely, and so it makes sense that we all take very individual approaches to life and its duties. We're all different—personalities, temperaments, perspectives, gifts, abilities, likes, dislikes, comfort zones, enthusiasms, tendencies, and reactions. And it is also good to keep in mind that there is no one right way to glorify God. We each reflect God's glory uniquely.

**1.** There really is one "one right way" we *should* mention. After that, though, you need to make allowances for differences. Take a look at John 14:6. What is the only way to come to God?

**2.** Do you ever wonder if, no matter what way you try to glorify God, you'll never be able to get things right? What words of comfort does Peter offer us in 2 Peter 1:3?

**3.** Okay, maybe there is one solid rule here. When it comes to our spiritual lives and glorifying God, the key is wholeheartedness. For instance, what does Jesus say we should do wholeheartedly in Mark 12:30?

**4.** Here's another one. What else do we need to give wholeheartedly to God, according to Proverbs 3:5?

> *As we meditate on God's Word, we become familiar with God's heart and His ways; as we do so, we will change. The purpose of meditation is not simply to let us feel good in a noisy world; it is not a self—absorbed agenda. Rather as we shut our mind in with God and reflect on His words, we will know Him and be changed by Him—and that is the purpose of our lives.*
>
> Sheila Walsh

**5.** Let's take on another wholehearted quality. These three verses will give you some perspective. What else does God ask of us in them?

- Why does David want understanding in Psalm 119:34?

- What does David say he will keep in Psalm 119:69?

- What must we earnestly do, according to Deuteronomy 11:13?

We all know there are things in life that have to be done, no matter how dull or unpleasant they might be. Those who can afford it pay others to do these tasks for them. Most of us, though, have to take care of them ourselves. There is no glory in these chores, and so they often become a drudgery. We come to resent having to do "servant's work" and being taken for granted. As we work, we mumble and grumble. What's more, we are tempted to approach these jobs half-heartedly, doing slipshod work, or even avoiding them altogether. It's called giving things a lick and a promise—just a quick dab and the promise to do a better job next time.

But have you realized that, when you pursue something with your whole heart, it does not become a drudgery? When we set our minds to do the task in front of us, when we give a job our full attention, when we do our work to the best of our ability, our efforts are rewarded. Even the most commonplace tasks present us with a way to bring glory to God. So shift your perspective—decide to approach life wholeheartedly. What kinds of things have become a drudgery to you—household chores, your job, your involvement at church, Bible reading, prayer? Don't just give them a lick and a promise. Do them with your whole heart!

> *You can do loving things with your own things today: organize a drawer, pick a bouquet of wildflowers, write in your journal, draw a picture card for a child, pat a puppy, braid a little girl's hair, make a batch of cookies, decorate a wall or shelf, pinch a cheek, pull some weeds, wash your husband's car. The boomerang in all this is that the hand that gives, gathers!*
>
> Barbara Johnson

**6.** What else can we do wholeheartedly, according to Psalm 119:58 and Psalm 119:145?

**7.** According to Psalm 111:1, what can we offer to the LORD with our whole hearts?

> *Paul encourages us to do whatever we do with all our hearts. He tells us to put our soul into it. Like the old song says, "You gotta have heart." When you do, you can do anything. The busiest days can become our most joyful.*
>
> Luci Swindoll

**8.** Samuel was a good and wise prophet of God. What does he call for the people of God to do in 1 Samuel 12:20, 24?

**9.** There is just one more wholehearted characteristic in this lesson. Take a look at these verses:

- How can we be sure to find God, according to Deuteronomy 4:29?
- What does God Himself tell us in Jeremiah 29:13?
- What does David call those who wholeheartedly seek the LORD in Psalm 119:2?

## ✦ DIGGING DEEPER ✦

When it comes to God, there is no half way. No middle of the road. No sitting on the fence. He wants our all. Take a look at Deuteronomy 10:12, 13. What does this verse say God requires of His people? Take a look:

*What does the LORD your God require of you, but to fear the LORD your God, to walk in all His ways and to love Him, to serve the LORD your God with all your heart and with all your soul, and to keep the commandments of the LORD and His statutes which I command you today for your good?*

## ✦ PONDER & PRAY ✦

There is no one right way to glorify God, because God asks different things of all of us. This week, why not spend some time pondering God's plans for you? What gifts has he given you? What opportunities do you have to use them? Then ask, too, for the strength to do the thing in front of you wholeheartedly. Give God your best, and He will receive the glory.

## ✦ TRINKETS TO TREASURE ✦

Ever find yourself singing that old song "All of me, why not take all of me? Can't you see, that I'm so lost without you?" Nothing could serve better for a trinket this week than a heart. Not half of a heart, not even most of a heart, but a whole heart, because the only way to glorify God is to do it wholeheartedly.

## ✦ NOTES & PRAYER REQUESTS ✦

## ✦ NOTES & PRAYER REQUESTS ✦

# CREDIT WHERE CREDIT IS DUE

"O MY SOUL, YOU HAVE SAID TO THE LORD, 'YOU ARE MY LORD, MY GOODNESS IS NOTHING APART FROM YOU."

**Psalm 16:2**

We learned what it means to glorify something in Lesson 1. When we glorify God, we acknowledge His excellence, give honor where honor is due, and praise Him for the things He has done. Now it's time to look at the verb "to glory." Glorying means triumphant rejoicing, exulting, boasting, and being proud about something. In the Bible, "to glory" is often translated "to boast." Now boasting isn't all bad. It depends on what you're boasting about—or "glorying in," to use the biblical terminology. I love that song Mr. Rogers used to sing, "I'm proud of me, so proud of me. I hope that you are proud of me too." When something goes well, comes out just right, or does just what it's supposed to do, we

## CLEARING + THE + COBWEBS

Which would you rather be known as— a strong, self-reliant, independent woman, or a quiet, submissive woman completely dependent on another?

know it. We would be edging into false humility if we tried to deny excellence when we see it. The LORD encourages us to do our best, doing our work "as unto the LORD." He is pleased when we do what we were made to do. Remember the story of Eric Liddell? He's the *Chariots of Fire* guy, and God made him fast. He's famous for saying "When I run, I feel God's pleasure."

What is your thing—the thing that, when done well, allows you to feel God's pleasure. Is it writing letters of encouragement, organizing an event, concocting the perfect pecan pie, reading storybooks with your grandchild, helping people learn how to manage their finances, weeding the flower beds, watercolor painting, playing softball, or keeping up with your friends? You can glory in the experience of a job well done, and by doing what God has made you to do, you please Him.

**1.** Jesus told stories to teach us valuable lessons for living. What does He tell us not to do in Matthew 6:2?

*Every day God reminds us to quit holding things too tightly—whether an event, a viewpoint, a desire, a particular time in life, or a person we thoroughly enjoy. He urges us to stop struggling, resisting, coercing, or manipulating for what we want. When we simply do what he asks, no matter how hard it seems, and we keep our focus on the Light of the world, an amazing brightness comes, all within the embrace of his love.*

Luci Swindoll

**2.** Glorying in ourselves is a short–lived pleasure, and glory isn't something we should snatch up or try to keep. What does 1 Peter 1:24 say about the glory of man?

**3.** So what is the alternative? Scripture offers us the perfect answer. Read Jeremiah 9:23, 24. What does God say we should not glory in? What should we do instead?

**4.** What is Paul's reason for glorying? He records it in Romans 15:17.

> *I want to know for myself what God says. I want to know the things that make Him happy and the things that break His heart. I want to know how to live a life that will please Him. How can I do that if I don't study His words to me?*
>
> Sheila Walsh

**5.** Take a look at John 7:18. In this passage, Jesus is talking about Himself, but what principle can we glean from what He says about seeking glory?

My sister and I are completely different body types. She's an apple and I'm a pear. Growing up, I rather prided myself for being slim (of waist anyhow). To get even, my sister nicknamed me "Thunder Thighs." It's become something of a family joke.

Remember Anne of Green Gables? Most girls seem to grow up with her as a friend through the books written about her. Poor Anne had a constant source of regret in her life—her red hair. How she longed to have hair the color of spun gold, or the glossy black of a raven's wing. Anything but red. However, Anne was able to rally her spirits a little because she knew she had a pretty nose. Having a pretty nose was a great comfort to her.

We compare ourselves, envy each other, and take comfort in our best features. As women, it is easy to slip into our little "glories." Sure, we have things we don't like about ourselves. "I can't wear pink." "My feet are too wide." "I can't grow my nails out." "My hair never cooperates." "My teeth aren't white enough." "I have thunder thighs." So to make us feel better about ourselves, we check out the gal next to us. "I'm glad my fingers aren't that short." "Look at her ankles." "At least I have two eyebrows." Oh my! And we glory in the little deficiencies we find simply because we do not share them.

Shame on us! All this cattiness is not acceptable in God's eyes. He wants us to get over ourselves. God doesn't want us to glory in our clear complexions, thick hair, slim waistlines, or pretty noses. Hear the message again: "Let him who glories glory in this, that he understands and knows Me, that I am the LORD" (Jer. 9:24).

**6.** True beauty in God's eyes comes from what, according to 1 Peter 3:3, 4?

> *I am so grateful Jesus enables me to change, one groaning effort at a time, and I'm thankful for those folks in my life who have given me the space and time to change.*
>
> Patsy Clairmont

**7.** Wealth, beauty, popularity, success, charisma, poise, good taste — all these things are recognized and applauded by the world. These are things in which we are expected to glory. By contrast, what are the characteristics of the woman who glories in the LORD, according to Psalm 64:10?

**8.** Have you ever read the description of the woman in Proverbs 31? Apparently, the ideal woman doesn't have to be much of a looker. What quality is considered praiseworthy—even better than charm and beauty?

*Being touched by God's extravagant grace ignites something within us that causes others to notice. It's an interior glow that is like an exterior light in that it casts its influence in spite of the degree of darkness in which it finds itself—not only in spite of the darkness but because of it. In the darkness the light becomes more attractive, more influential, more valuable, and more obvious.*

Patsy Clairmont

**9.** A beautiful woman glories in her beauty. Yet true beauty is found in the spirit. A rich man glories in his riches. Yet where are true riches found, according to Matthew 6:19, 20?

**10.** We cannot snatch at glory. Borrowed glory is quick to fade. The message of this chapter is worth repeating again, because as simple as it is, it is hard to live out. What does Paul repeat in 2 Corinthians 10:17, 18?

## ✦ DIGGING DEEPER ✦

In Romans 15:17, Paul says he gloried in the things that pertain to God. Have you ever stopped to ponder what these things might be? In 1 Peter 3:3, 4, Peter reminds his audience they have been given everything they need pertaining to life and godliness. Take a look at this same passage as it is translated in *The Message*. What does Peter say Jesus has provided for us?

*Everything that goes into a life of pleasing God has been miraculously given to us by getting to know, personally and intimately, the One who invited us to God. The best invitation we ever received! We were also given absolutely terrific promises to pass on to you — your tickets to participation in the life of God after you turned your back on a world corrupted by lust.*

## ✦ PONDER & PRAY ✦

Glory is not something we can hang onto. We are meant to return it to God. And those of us who are tempted to glory in temporary things are being unwise and even foolish. We are to glory in God. There is nothing else worth boasting about. In your times of prayer this week, ask the LORD to help you stay honest with yourself and with Him. Ask Him to teach you how to glory in Him, rather than in yourself.

# ✦ TRINKETS TO TREASURE ✦

What do we have to boast about? Where is our treasure? The only things that last are in God's hands. This week's trinket is a little treasure box. It isn't big enough to hold all your valuables, but it can remind you of what your true treasure is. Not wealth. Not beauty. Not the praise and admiration of others. Our true treasure awaits us in heaven, and the only thing we can glory in is God.

## ✦ NOTES & PRAYER REQUESTS ✦

CHAPTER 8

# GLORIOUS WORSHIP

### "SING OUT THE HONOR OF HIS NAME; MAKE HIS PRAISE GLORIOUS."

**Psalm 66:2**

When some people think of glorifying God, the first thing that comes to mind is a big corporate worship service. There's a very good reason for this! The worship services we attend in our churches are designed to pull the focus off of ourselves and onto the God we serve. They give us the chance to unite together with one voice and tell God how much we love Him. We sing of God's great power, His mighty deeds, and His grace and mercy. As we sing, we tell God how grateful we are His love, forgiveness, and hope. We have songs that commemorate the events in Jesus' life— His birth, His sacrifice, His Resurrection, and His imminent return. Through song, we rehearse the basics of our beliefs, reminding ourselves of the truths found in

## CLEARING
### ✦ THE ✦
## COBWEBS

Do you have a favorite worship song you've heard on the radio, cassette tape, or CD? Maybe you have a favorite song you sing in church? Which one is it?

Scripture. In singing, we recommit ourselves to follow Him with faithfulness, to trust Him completely, and to be used for His glory.

There are the songs we are taught from the very beginning—"Jesus Loves Me," "The B–I–B–L–E," "Jesus Loves the Little Children," and "My God is So Big" There are great old hymns of the faith—"The Old Rugged Cross," "O, For a Thousand Tongues to Sing," "It Is Well," and "Amazing Grace." There are praise choruses that have become precious—"Because He Lives," "As the Deer," "Majesty," and "Jesus, Name Above All Names." And new songs are added every year— "Awesome God," "Shout to the LORD," "Draw Me Close," and "Agnus Dei."

Songs—old and new—give us the opportunity to raise our voices in worship—glorious worship.

**1.** How is singing described by David in Psalm 27:6? What stirred up this desire to sing in the first place?

*When you're going through your daily routine or when you face trials and tribulations, do you allow music to comfort you? When times are good, do you stop to sing for joy? God enjoys the song we lift up in praise to Him.*

Thelma Wells

**2.** What causes the saints to break into song, according to Psalm 149:5?

**3.** How do believers glorify God together, according to Paul in Romans 15:6?

**4.** How does the psalmist describe the praise of the upright in Psalm 33:1–3?

> *Our family enjoys good gospel music. We have discovered that praising God in song lifts our spirits, clears our heads, and opens a place for the Holy Spirit to speak to us.*
>
> Thelma Wells

**5.** Where is God when the worship is going on, according to Psalm 22:3?

I love to hear certain worship tapes when I do my housework. Even my kids know when I put in certain CDs, it's time to do some serious cleaning. The music is upbeat, fun to sing along to, and seems to automatically put me into a cheerful frame of mind. It's much more fun to dust when you're dancing inside! It's true that

Christian music can put us in a happier mood, but singing the songs doesn't necessarily mean we are worshiping God. Let me try to explain. Take one of your favorite songs. Do you love it because the melody line is catchy? Do you sing it because it makes you happy? Do you like the rhythm, which sets your foot to tapping? Do you enjoy harmonizing with the other voices? Do you pop the CD into the car stereo to help you through rush hour frustrations? Do you know the song so well you can sing it without giving the words a second thought? Hey, me too! Unfortunately, not one of those reasons has anything to do with God. Do you understand the meaning of the words you're singing? Often we are singing for our own enjoyment, not for God's pleasure.

Glorifying God only happens when we put Him first: first in our thoughts, first in our decisions, and first in our plans. Don't just go through the motions of worship. Don't just go with the flow. Don't be in it for the experience alone or the emotional high. Be intentional in your worship, and keep it focused on your LORD and God. Engage your mind when you sing. Think about the words. Consider what they mean. Say them. Sing them to God. Mean it.

6. Habakkuk 3:3 says God's glory "covered the heavens, and the earth was full of His praise." What should be the topic of our praise, according to Psalm 138:5?

**7.** What does Psalm 29:1, 2 say we should give to the LORD?

**8.** Part of the beauty of worship is telling God about Himself. We do this by acknowledging His attributes. In biblical terminology, we "ascribe" things to God. What do these verses say can be ascribed to God?

- Deuteronomy 32:3

- Job 36:3

- Psalm 68:34

**9.** Psalm 71:8 says, "Let my mouth be filled with Your praise And with Your glory all the day." What two reasons are given later in Psalm 71:22–24 for lifting our voice in song?

> *We have to stand in the complexity of all that God is working on, not just in the simple part we can see for ourselves.*
>
> Nicole Johnson

## ✦ DIGGING DEEPER ✦

The psalms are filled with words of worship. Many of these written songs have been put to music, so the psalms are still sung today in our churches. Take a look at these verses. All of them talk about worship and praise and songs of rejoicing.

- Psalm 66:4
- Psalm 66:8
- Psalm 69:30
- Psalm 71:23

## ✦ PONDER & PRAY ✦

In the week ahead, make a concerted effort to add singing to your days. Choose songs of worship, songs that ascribe greatness to God, songs that are prayers. Sing while you are in the car, while you are busy around the house, and in the shower. Give voice to your prayers through music, and mean every word of it.

## ✦ TRINKETS TO TREASURE ✦

This week's lesson has been all about making beautiful music for the LORD, so you'll need something melodious for your trinket. How about a bird whistle? These little children's toys are often shaped like birds, and when you fill them with water and blow, they twitter and burble prettily. Lift up your voices and your whistles to the glory of the LORD this week.

## ✦ Notes & Prayer Requests ✦

## ✦ Notes & Prayer Requests ✦

# CHAPTER 9

# GREATER GLORIES

"I PRAY FOR THEM. I DO NOT PRAY FOR THE WORLD BUT
FOR THOSE WHOM YOU HAVE GIVEN ME, FOR THEY ARE
YOURS. AND ALL MINE ARE YOURS, AND YOURS ARE
MINE, AND I AM GLORIFIED IN THEM."

**John 17:9, 10**

Sometimes it feels as if our Christian walk wouldn't be so difficult if life didn't keep getting in the way. It's the same thing on Sunday mornings. Sometimes, we feel as if the worship service just goes on and on. Corporate worship is glorious, but at some point, we have to leave the pew and exit the sanctuary. We *want* to glorify God, but life is busy, our schedules are packed, there are bills to be paid, projects due at the office, and we can't just set it all aside for an hour or two of quiet reflection every day.

Whoops! Hold the phone! Wait a minute! Who ever said we need large blocks of time carved out of our schedules for quiet reflection? That's how we think,

## CLEARING
## ✦ THE ✦
## COBWEBS

Do you have Bible verses hanging on the walls anywhere in your house— pictures, plaques, and post–it notes? Which passages are they?

though. We take a look at our schedule and say, "Okay, God. I'll give you three hours on Sunday morning, one hour Sunday evening, and I can manage every other Wednesday night. I'll be checking in with you for fifteen minutes each morning and evening (unless I fall asleep), and a brief acknowledgement before each meal. Is that good for You? Great! I'll pencil you in." You see, we try to divide God's time from the rest of everyday life. This is God's time, holy and set apart for Him, and this is when I get everything else done.

But we don't have to pull ourselves out of living in order to glorify God. On the contrary! God doesn't want to be given designated sections of our day. He wants to be a part of every moment of your day! Don't relegate God to some corner. Let Him infuse your day with His strength, His patience, and His love. You will be a different woman for it, and He will get all the glory for the change in you!

**1.** Our times of worship bring glory to God, but there are greater glories to be had—the glory of a life lived for the LORD. God expects us to make Him a part of everyday living. This was always God's plan, as we can see in Deuteronomy 6:4–9. What did He tell His people to do and when?

> *I tell the LORD in prayer I will do whatever He asks of me. Then He sends some rascals into my life, and I'm irritated. When I said "whatever," I guess I meant as long as it's not too inconvenient, not too disruptive to my schedule, and not too long–term costly. The truth is, my "Whatever, LORD" is really more of a "However, LORD." "I'll do it, LORD; however, could you make it another time, a little easier, a more agreeable person, and to my liking?"*

Patsy Clairmont

**2.** What do we imagine when we think of giving glory to God—singing, preaching, giving testimonies, writing psalms? And yet, the Scriptures are filled with other ways of bringing glory to God—ways that are a little unexpected. Take a look at these:

- In John 11:4, what does Jesus say will bring glory to God?

- How does 1 Peter 4:14 say God can be glorified?

- In John 21:19, how did Jesus say Peter would end up glorifying God?

**3.** Shame, insults, sickness, and death are hardly the means we would choose for ourselves, even if we did want to glorify God. But many believers are asked by God to endure these things. They can glean encouragement from Paul in 2 Corinthians 4:17. Why does he say this hard path is still a good one?

**4.** How else is God's glory spread, according to Psalm 66:16?

> *God is interested in the tiniest things in the world. He cares about us and what we consider important. He gives us the desires of our hearts. He completes what He begins. He knows us by name.*
>
> Luci Swindoll

**5.** What can we tell others, according to Psalm 145:11?

**6.** What else brings praise and glory to God, according to Paul in Philippians 1:11?

Sometimes I think I'd like to pack my bags, kiss my responsibilities goodbye, and move into a monastery. It would be a quiet retreat—a time of refreshment, refocusing, and revitalization. I could live a simple existence in my own little cloister room. Distractions done away with, I could go about the business of things pertaining to God. I could begin a prayer journal. I could study the Bible for hours, uninterrupted. It would be so peaceful. It would be so quiet. I like quiet.

Unfortunately, God hasn't called any of us to be hermits. We were made to need one another. A life characterized by the fruit of the spirit is a life lived in the midst of fellow believers. We need these gifts of the Spirit just to get along! Besides, it is our great love and care for one another that sets us apart from the rest of the world. "All people will know that you are my followers if you love each other" (John 13:35 NCV).

**7.** There are more ways God is glorified through our lives. How does Paul say God was glorified through Abraham's life, according to Romans 4:20?

**8.** In the face of persecution and death, Paul says God's grace will cause what to abound? And what will be the result of that abundance? Read 2 Corinthians 4:15 for the answer.

**9.** What does Paul ask us to pray for in 2 Thessalonians 3:1? What does he want to see glorified?

> *In a culture where we all but worship activity and accomplishment, we can so easily miss time alone with God.*
>
> Luci Swindoll

**10.** Peter calls Christians to glorify God with their lives. What does he urge in 1 Peter 4:11?

## ✦ DIGGING DEEPER ✦

Though most of us have never had to face such things, Christians around the world are subjected to persecution for their faith. God's people are promised they will suffer because of Jesus (John 15:20), but the suffering will bring glory to God. Take a look at these passages, which give encouragement to believers in the midst of tribulations:

- Romans 5:3–5
- 1 Peter 1:7
- 2 Timothy 2:10
- 1 Peter 5:10

## ✦ PONDER & PRAY ✦

Glory comes in more forms than you might think, and most of them are not musical! Our worship might be glorious, but what happens when the music fades? Pray this week for God to show you how to keep from compartmentalizing Him out of the mainstream of your days. Ask God to help you weave your day around His plans, integrating praise, prayer, meditation, Scripture, and the Spirit's promptings with your usual responsibilities.

## ✦ TRINKETS TO TREASURE ✦

This week's gift is a piece of rough, woven cloth—not unlike the stuff a monk's robes would be made of. But this fabric isn't meant to nudge you in the direction of sacred solitude. On the contrary, the interwoven threads of the cloth are to remind you how God has called you to use your gifts in the church, weaving your life into the lives of other believers. Your life is knit together with that of the Spirit. It is His presence that gives us the strength and patience to minister to other believers.

## ✦ NOTES & PRAYER REQUESTS ✦

## ✦ NOTES & PRAYER REQUESTS ✦

# CHAPTER 10

# EVERYDAY GLORIES

### "I BLESS GOD EVERY CHANCE I GET; MY LUNGS EXPAND WITH HIS PRAISE."

**Psalm 34:1** MSG

We know all about everyday things. We have everyday clothes—our "grungies" we wear when we clean house, join the kids in the sand box, and mow the lawn. We have everyday shoes—well worn, and comfy. We have everyday hairstyles—wash and wear, out of the way, no fuss–no muss. We have everyday dishes—dishwasher safe and durable, where only a few are chipped. Everyday stuff is the stuff we use all the time. Everyday stuff is ordinary, normal, run–of–the–mill, basic, average, typical, commonplace, and routine. Most of the time, we think that everyday things are really kind of dull—humdrum, mundane, even boring.

## CLEARING ✦ THE ✦ COBWEBS

Do you have two sets of dishes—one for everyday use and one for special occasions? How often do you use the good dishes?

> *Life is mostly just getting in the car or on another airplane, climbing the steps to one platform at a time, and faithfully holding God's picture in place—whether I feel like it or not. As we do the thing in front of us, joy comes.*
>
> Barbara Johnson

But when we're getting ready to go out, or when we're having company, that's when we get out the good stuff. We take out the dry–clean–only dresses, spend time in front of a mirror on our hair, slip into a pair of leather pumps, and lay out the fine china. When we know other people will be seeing us, we want to put on our best face. And that's what we should be giving God—our best. Are we giving God our best?

The concept we've been trying to get across in this study is that giving glory to God is not a "special occasion." You don't have to get into your Sunday best, drive to the nearest sanctuary, and be led by a worship team in order to praise God. Giving God glory comes in all ways, shapes, and forms, and it's something that happens every day. God wants to be a part of your normal, ordinary, run of the mill, everyday routine.

**1.** When it comes to everyday glories, just what kinds of things *should* we be doing every day—the kinds of things that will bring glory to God's name? Take a look at these Scriptures, which showcase some of the actions and attitudes that must characterize our lives:

    • Why don't we need to worry about our lives, according to Philippians 4:19?


    • What were the believers in Acts 17:11 known for?

• What can we trust God to do, according to Psalm 31:3?

• What has God provided us with, according to 2 Peter 1:3?

• Psalm 69:13 concentrates on what everyday activity?

• What should we do with the Scriptures, according to Deuteronomy 30:14?

**2.** The life of a believer is far from flashy. What should our aspirations be, according to 1 Thessalonians 4:11?

**3.** How does Paul describe the lives of Christians in 1 Timothy 2:2?

> *I have learned that sometimes we will be aware of God's closeness and sometimes we won't. At times we experience the sweetness of God's nearness and at other times the frightening loneliness of His distance. The LORD hasn't changed locations, but we might have been caught up in our own agendas and forgotten His presence and availability.*
>
> Patsy Clairmont

**4.** The quiet life is quite a theme in the Scriptures. What does God say will bring us strength, according to Isaiah 30:15?

**5.** When we lead a quiet life, we're able to see and hear some things more clearly.

    • What does God ask of us in Psalm 46:10?

    • Why does being quiet help us to hear God's voice in spite of distractions, according to 1 Kings 19:12?

    • When you are paying attention to God, what will you be able to hear, according to Isaiah 30:21?

What does it mean to be "full-time"? Most people who punch the clock with full-time jobs can expect to work eight hours a day, with a half hour thrown in for lunch. Some people who work full-time are salaried, and they often put in sixty hours a week. Others who have full-time jobs put in their hours, but are "on call." They have to drop everything and come whenever they are needed. Mothers are full-time no matter what their other responsibilities might be, working from dawn to dusk and on–call all night long. Then, there are those we call "full–time Christian workers." They are the pastors, evangelists, missionaries — people whose only job is wrapped up in the church and in the spreading of the gospel.

So if they're full–time Christians, does that mean the rest of us are just part–timers? Do you punch out on Sundays as you leave the church? Do you pass the buck on big projects — Bible reading, Bible study, hospitality, visitation, and prayer — to the ones whose *job* it is to do them? We shouldn't let such attitudes slip unnoticed into our heart. We're all full–time Christians!

> *In this crazy world it's nice to know that some people still perform commonplace work with dignity, holding the world together with old–fashioned, down–home virtues.*
>
> Barbara Johnson

**6.** Here is a beautiful passage of praise from Psalm 51:15–17, 19. What does David say God desires from us?

**7.** As in any relationship, things go both ways. We are asked to live faithfully before God, to listen for His voice through the Word, and to have a teachable heart. But God is also glorified in our lives when He does certain things for us. What does 2 Corinthians 1:20 say God does to His own glory?

**8.** And here's one more. What does John 14:13 say we are given, to the glory of God?

## ✦ DIGGING DEEPER ✦

David asked God for everyday things all the time. The psalms are filled with prayers asking God to make Himself a very real part of David's days. Take this passage from the Psalms and turn it into your own prayer—an everyday kind of prayer.

> *Show me Your ways, O LORD; teach me Your paths. Lead me in Your truth and teach me, For You are the God of my salvation; On You I wait all the day. Good and upright is the LORD; Therefore He teaches sinners in the way. The humble He guides in justice, And the humble He teaches His way. All the paths of the LORD are mercy and truth, To such as keep His covenant and His testimonies. For Your name's sake, O LORD, Pardon my iniquity, for it is great.* —Psalm 25:4, 5, 8–11

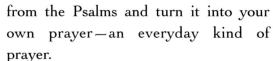

*When we get away from the invasive noise and activity of this world that makes so many demands on our time and attention, when we tune into our relationship with Christ, we discover the wonder that we are waiting for. We can wait for wonder to come knocking at our door. But if we will be quiet and listen, we will hear it knocking at our hearts.*

Sheila Walsh

## ✦ PONDER & PRAY ✦

You may not be able to slow down the hectic pace of your workplace, and your home may be filled with noisy children, but ask God to help you find quietness this week in a quiet heart, a quieted mind, and a quiet and teachable spirit. Ask the Spirit to tune your ears, so you can recognize the LORD's call and follow Him down paths of truth. God will teach you the way if you ask Him.

## ✦ TRINKETS TO TREASURE ✦

The Christian life is filled with everyday, commonplace things, and God wants to be made a part of them. It may not be exciting by the world's standards, but a quiet life is free from worry and can boast answered prayers and kept promises. This week's trinket is a pin, to remind you, when you quiet your heart enough to hear a pin drop, then you'll be able to listen to the leading God gives.

## ✦ NOTES & PRAYER REQUESTS ✦

Lincoln Park - Crisis Pregnancy Center

June 10. Mom's 9:AM.

Legacy Hope - Retired Missionaries

# CHAPTER 11

# INTENTIONAL DAYS

### "THE WISDOM THAT IS FROM ABOVE IS FIRST PURE, THEN PEACEABLE, GENTLE, WILLING TO YIELD, FULL OF MERCY AND GOOD FRUITS, WITHOUT PARTIALITY AND WITHOUT HYPOCRISY."

**James 3:17**

'm a to–do list kind of gal. If it's not down on paper, I'll probably forget it! Grocery lists, honey–do lists, reading lists, Christmas lists, wish lists, "don't forget to…" lists, and the list of errands I need to run this afternoon. Being list oriented, I don't like to do something and not get credit for it. I'll often add things to my list after I've done them, just to have the satisfaction of crossing them off! Sitting down and making lists helps me to stay focused. This can be vitally important, especially when grocery shopping. You might drop into the local market, knowing you need just a few things, but by the time you've reached the checkout counter, the cart is piled with several

## CLEARING
## ✦ THE ✦
## COBWEBS

What kinds of things do you think about when your mind wanders?

*Letters of Kevin Young*

tempting treats and you've forgotten what you came for in the first place.

That's the way our days can go as well. We might start out in the morning knowing we need to glorify God with our lives and include Him in our days. But once we get going, there are so many little distractions. By the time the sun has set, we find we've frittered away our day without giving the LORD a thought.

> Don't let your life speed out of control. Live intentionally. Do something today that will last beyond your lifetime.
>
> Barbara Johnson

If we're going to include God in our days, we can't expect it to just happen. Good intentions never get things done. In this lesson, let's look at the Scriptures that talk about living intentionally, and wisely. The Scriptures use phrases like "set your mind," and "purpose in your heart," and "order your ways." Nowadays, we'd say we need to make up our minds, plan ahead, stick to the routine, and get into the habit of hanging out with God—every day.

**1.** Let's begin with Proverbs 16:20. Who will find good? Who will be happy?

**2.** Every good plan starts with research. If you intend to live for God's glory, the Scriptures are your starting point. What does 1 John 3:22 say we should be doing?

**3.** To put it another way, look at the words of Jesus in John 14:15. What will a follower of Jesus do if she loves Him?

**4.** There's no way to straddle the fence in spiritual matters. With God, it's all or nothing. What does Romans 6:16 call us? What are our two choices?

**5.** We can choose. We must choose. What does Paul say is the wisest course, according to Colossians 3:2?

> *There are days when I'm so busy living life I don't take time to feel anything. I just go along without thought, trying to get things done. I hate days like that—plodding through duties without being conscious. No sense of purpose. Frankly, I fight that feeling because it's important for me to live fully every moment whenever possible.*
>
> Luci Swindoll

**6.** So can we make a to–do list for ourselves? "Item number one: Glorify God today. Item number two: Study the Scripture to find out what will please God. Item number three: Obey God." We like lists. In fact, I'll bet you've memorized a few of them. Take a look at these Scripture passages: *Beatitudes*

• Matthew 5:3–12

• Galatians 5:22, 23 *Fruit of the Spirit all of them*

• Philippians 4:8

*H*ave you ever noticed how literal children can be? It can be funny, or it can be frustrating, but it's always interesting to see how their minds work. I was once sitting at the breakfast table with a bunch of people when a daddy in our group asked his little girl how she had slept. Without missing a beat, she tipped her head sideways, closed her eyes, and started to snore lightly. We all got a laugh out of her literal response.

But there are times when the literal approach can become frustrating. For instance, when I tell my sons the family room needs tidying, I'll often say something like, "Look at this mess! Boys, pick up your Legos®." They'll come to me in a while to tell me they're done, and I'll go check on their work. Sure enough, all the Legos® will be safely stowed in their basket. But there will still be books, magazines, and stuffed animals lying around. When I point this out, they'll say innocently, "But you only said to pick up the Legos®." Such is human nature!

I think that's why God never gave us a checklist. God doesn't say, "If you do this thing and this thing and this thing, then you're covered." You see, lists come with loopholes. That's what the Pharisees tried to do, and Jesus called them a brood of vipers! Instead, our instructions are left very open–ended. God has told us to trust Him and to obey Him. To live this way is to live wisely.

> *When we ask for wisdom, all kinds of things begin to happen. Things we hadn't planned on. God comes in like a flood, altering our world—changing the things we once valued, restructuring relationships, taking away this desire and adding that one, putting our priorities in a new alignment. God grows us up!*
>
> Luci Swindoll

7. With God's Word as our guide, we can make right choices. We can choose to live wisely. Match the chapter and verse in Proverbs to the characteristic of a wise person found there.

| | | |
|---|---|---|
| *d* Proverbs 1:5 | a. teachable |
| *a* Proverbs 9:9 | b. able to keep emotions in check |
| *g* Proverbs 10:19 | c. avoids temptation |
| *h* Proverbs 11:30 | d. always learning |
| *f* Proverbs 13:20 | e. accepts correction |
| *c* Proverbs 14:16 | f. chooses wise friends |
| *e* Proverbs 17:10 | g. knows when to be silent |
| *b* Proverbs 29:11 | h. wins people to the Lord |

**8.** Do you feel like you're still lacking wisdom? Never fear! There's a Bible verse for that, too! Take a look at James 1:5. What does it promise?

## ✦ DIGGING DEEPER ✦

Let's go back to Philippians today, and consider this list from Paul's pen.

*Whatever things are true, whatever things are noble, whatever things are just, whatever things are pure, whatever things are lovely, whatever things are of good report, if there is any virtue and if there is anything praiseworthy—meditate on these things.* — Philippians 4:8

Take a few minutes to turn this into an actual list. These are the kinds of things Paul was talking about when he urged us to set our minds on things above—godly things, holy things. Why not make this list the basis for your prayer today. Apply each phrase to yourself, and hide it in your heart. Bend your mind in God's direction, and choose to ponder on these things in the days to come.

## ✦ PONDER & PRAY ✦

Take a few minutes, and write out a Scripture prayer based on Philippians 4:8 here. *Thank you Lord for My church and the good people there who always encourage, thank you God for bringing me there, to that particular church, to learn your Word and how to apply it. Thank you Lord for the teachings that are discussed for learning for living, and for loving my fellow Christians as we go through this life watching and learning more about you through the Word. Thank you Lord for all the good people you have put in my life. Amen.*

## ✦ TRINKETS TO TREASURE ✦

We must be wise in our choices and intentional with our time if we are going to live a life to the glory of God. To remind ourselves of these things, our trinket this week will borrow from the old cliché, "wise old owl." (I like it better than the more biblical "wise as serpents.") Let the little guy help you keep your thoughts winging upwards, for it's there we need to set them—on things above.

## ✦ Notes & Prayer Requests ✦

# CHAPTER 12

# LIVING FOR HIS GLORY

## "WITH GOODWILL DOING SERVICE, AS TO THE LORD, AND NOT TO MEN."

### Ephesians 6:7

*I* have always had a fascination with butlers. If I could manage it, I'd hire a good, old–fashioned English butler in a heartbeat. Can't you just see some dignified older gentleman in a smart suit? Butlers are always proper, always pleasant, always polite. Their entire purpose in life is to serve—to be at your every beck and call. A good butler knows what you need even before you do. With the whisper of gloved hands, fresh water glasses appear and old ones are whisked away. Butlers act on your behalf, answering the doorbell and sending for the car. They are unobtrusive—gliding through a room full of guests as if invisible, and fading away when their work is done. Yet

## CLEARING ✦ THE ✦ COBWEBS

Butlers show up in literature a lot, especially in the old English countryside mysteries. That's why we still say, "The butler did it." Personally, I'm fond of Alfred—Bruce Wayne's butler. Do you have a favorite butler?

when you need them again, they're right there at your elbow. The fascinating thing about these butlers is they never seem to want or need praise for what they do. They accept their role as servant, and even take pride in fulfilling their role without being noticed. You'd never catch a butler drawing attention to himself—"Hey, look at me! Didn't I do that well? Isn't my timing superb?" No! That would be undignified, unbecoming, not the "done thing."

> *When we trust God outside of our comfort zones, anything can happen, anywhere. And sometimes what happens is utterly delightful.*
>
> Luci Swindoll

So when I think of living out my life for God's glory, as a quiet and gentle Christian woman, I have this ideal in my head. I want to model my behavior after two people: Jesus and the English butler. I want to model myself after Jesus, for His focus, His compassion, and His dependence upon the Father. And the butler for his quietness, his readiness to serve, and for his humility.

**1.** As always, Jesus leads the way. Take a look at the role He filled while on earth:

- What does God the Father call Jesus in Matthew 12:18? *His Servant*

- What does Mark 10:45 say was Jesus' purpose in coming? *For even the Son of Man came not to be served but to serve, and to give His life as a ransom for many.*

- In Luke 22:27, how does Jesus describe his position to the disciples? *As a servant, not to be regarded as the greatest*

**2.** What does Jesus say in John 12:26 to those who want to follow His example and become servants of Christ? *If anyone serves me, he must follow me; and where I am, there will my servant be also. If anyone serves me, the Father will honor him.*

**3.** How does Paul say we should offer ourselves for God's service, according to Romans 12:1? *To present our bodies as a living sacrifice, holy and acceptable to God, which is your spiritual worship.*

**4.** Here are a few verses that talk about some of God's service requirements:

- Whom shall we serve, according to Matthew 4:10? *"You shall worship the Lord your God, and Him only shall you serve."*

- Whom does Paul say we serve in Colossians 3:24? *You are serving the Lord Christ.*

- What point does Jesus make very clear in Matthew 6:24? *No one can serve two masters; for either he will hate the one and love the other. You cannot serve God and money.*

e don't bring honor to our Heavenly Father because of our glowing countenances or gleaming halos. That's for the angels to do. But our faithfulness brings glory to God. In fact, the angels are fascinated by our lives. We're probably better than a soap opera, with all the ups and downs we experience! But they're rooting for us. They are amazed at how we love Jesus, whom we have not seen. They are thrilled to see us choose to serve God, in spite of our sinful state. And they rejoice over us when we remain faithful, despite all odds. Our complete dependence on God is cause to celebrate and to give God the glory for His perfect plan of redemption.

> *I began to realize that one of my most annoying problems was me. That was painfully revealing. How could I be my own problem? Simple: I wanted control. Control of everything! I resented the fact that God wanted control too. My desire for control outweighed my desire for connectedness, even with Him.*
>
> Luci Swindoll

**5.** Sometimes we can pick up tidbits of information from phrases here and there in the Bible. How does Paul describe his relationship to God in Acts 27:23? And in Romans 1:9, how does Paul describe his service to God? *For this very night there stood before me an angel of the Lord to whom I belong and whom I worship. For God is my witness, whom I serve with my spirit in the gospel of his Son*

**6.** Jesus says, "If anyone desires to be first, he shall be last of all and servant of all" (Mark 9:35). Paul certainly took this to heart. What does he say he has done in 1 Corinthians 9:19? *If anyone would be first, he must be last of all and servant of all.*

**7.** Luke 17:9 says, "Does he [the master] thank that servant because he did the things that were commanded him? I think not." You don't get brownie points for doing something you're supposed to do anyhow. But when a servant shows integrity in doing her job, even when the master is away—that's another matter! What does Matthew 24:46 call such a person? And what commendation will she receive, according to Matthew 25:21? *24:46 - Blessed is that servant whom his master will find so doing when he comes. 25: 21 - Well done good and faithful servant; you have been faithful over a little; I will set you over much. Enter into the joy of your master.*

**8.** When the time comes for us to leave this earth and see our Heavenly Father face to face, I hope we can echo the words of Christ. What did He say in John 17:4, just before facing the Cross? *I glorified you on earth, having accomplished the work that you gave me to do.*

## ✦ DIGGING DEEPER ✦

Take a look at Jesus' words to His twelve disciples in John 15:15. What has changed for them? What does this mean for us?

*No longer do I call you servants, for a servant does not know what his master is doing; but I have called you friends, for all things that I heard from My Father I have made known to you.* — John 15:15

## ✦ PONDER & PRAY ✦

This week, as you finish this study on glorifying God in everyday living, take the time to go back over the past twelve weeks. Ponder through the Scripture passages, and pray for the LORD to show you how to take hold of them and put them to use in your life. Ask God to help you weave your life into His, so as you go forward in His service, He will be glorified.

## ✦ TRINKETS TO TREASURE ✦

You want to serve the LORD, and this week's lesson invites you to do it with a touch of class. You don't need to be a butler to serve God well, but you can display the same qualities we associate with those dapper menservants — willing, pleasant, dignified, and humble. So your trinket for this week is a pair of white gloves. Don them with pride, and find ways to serve the LORD in ways only He will notice. Even in quiet ways, God will be glorified by your faithful service.

## ✦ NOTES & PRAYER REQUESTS ✦

Lord, please help me to keep my white gloves spotless by serving you and you only.

Prayer for Bonnie and Jim Gill; For Nancy and Steve Bayrai; For my son, Jim, and his family in the way his son Zacharey is living his life away from you. He confessed his faith in You when he was younger, but the world has pulled him in to sin and denial.

## ✦ SHALL WE REVIEW? ✦

**Every chapter has added a new trinket to your treasure trove of memories. Let's remind ourselves of the lessons they hold for us!**

 ### 1. Rice.

A humble enough grain, until it is glorified. Your handful of rice serves to remind you of how all glory belongs to God. Glory is His to give, and when it is given, we need to return it to Him.

 ### 2. A gold coin.

God is more precious than silver and more costly than gold. We glorify God because it is due Him. This trinket is meant to point us to God and remind us that He alone is worthy of glory.

 ### 3. A star.

The heavens declare God's glory, and so can we. This little treasure serves to remind us of our purpose to bring God glory, so keep on twinkling, little star!

### 4. A clock.

When do we give glory to God? This little gift is our reminder that all of our days belong to God, and every hour and minute and moment offers an opportunity to glorify Him. So make every second count!

### 5. An apple.

Sometimes we wish we could serve God on a grand scale. We long to do big things for Him, but more often than not He's asking us to be faithful in the little things of life. This trinket is a reminder that we can't rush spiritual fruit and we should avoid the temptation to tie false apples on our branches, pretending to be something we're not.

### 6. A heart.

We all have such unique gifts and places in the body of Christ it's difficult to establish a set rule for service. So the only right way to glorify God with our lives is to serve Him wholeheartedly.

### 7. A treasure box.

In this world, beauty and riches provide great temptations for us, but when it comes to glorying, we must glory in the LORD. Our treasure box is a reminder that our true treasures wait for us in heaven.

### 8. A bird whistle.

What a great reminder of how voices and music can be lifted together in glorious worship.

### 9. Woven cloth.

Our lives are interwoven with those of other believers, and when we use our gifts within the church, God is glorified. What's more, our lives are interwoven with God's through the Spirit, and it is His strength and patience and love that allow us to minister to one another.

## 10. A pin.

As Christians, we aspire to a quiet life and everyday glories, with God as an active participant in our days. When we quiet our hearts and settle our minds, we can hear a pin drop—and hear the still, small voice of God leading us in His ways.

## 11. An owl.

If we are to live for God's glory, we must set about it in intentional ways. This trinket is a reminder that we must be wise in our decisions, choosing to set our minds on things above.

## 12. White gloves.

You can take up this part of the butler's uniform, as a reminder of how our part is that of a servant. Your life is spent entirely for God. Your willingness to serve, your cheerful service, your faithful obedience, your readiness to act on His behalf—all bring glory to His name.

# ✦ Leader's Guide ✦

## Chapter 1

**1.** "Give to the LORD the glory due His name; Bring an offering, and come before Him. Oh, worship the LORD in the beauty of holiness!" (1 Chr. 16:29). We worship the LORD because of the beauty of His holiness. But remember! We give Him glory because it is due to Him. He gets the glory because His deserves it!

**2.** d, c, e, a, b

**3.** "For He received from God the Father honor and glory when such a voice came to Him from the Excellent Glory: 'This is My beloved Son, in whom I am well pleased'" (2 Pet. 1:17). God said, "That's My Boy!" and expressed His pleasure in Jesus' obedience.

**4.** "Who being the brightness of His glory and the express image of His person, and upholding all things by the word of His power, when He had by Himself purged our sins, sat down at the right hand of the Majesty on high" (Heb. 1:3). Jesus is called "the brightness of God's glory." In *The Message*, that phrase is translated, "The Son perfectly mirrors God, and is stamped with God's nature." He's the very image of God, and just as worthy of glory. And this is nothing new. Jesus has had great glory since before the world ever was (John 17:5).

**5.** "Jesus spoke these words, lifted up His eyes to heaven, and said: 'Father, the hour has come. Glorify Your Son, that Your Son also may glorify You'" (John 17:1). When God glorifies us, it is so we will in turn give glory back to Him. It's a part of our relationship with an amazing Heavenly Father.

**6.** "So also Christ did not glorify Himself to become High Priest, but it was He who said to Him: 'You are My Son, Today I have begotten You'" (Heb. 5:5). Jesus didn't have great ambitions and a plan to make it into the spotlight. He didn't try to glorify Himself. He let God do the glorifying.

**7.** "What is man that You are mindful of him, And the son of man that You visit him? For You have made him a little lower than the angels, And You have crowned him with glory and honor. You have made him to have dominion over the works of Your hands" (Ps. 8:4–6). In this verse, David shares his wonder at the realization of what God thinks about us, visits us, and gives us a place of great prominence in all of creation. But that wasn't enough. God finished His work by crowning us with glory and honor.

**8.** "The LORD will give grace and glory; No good thing will He withhold from those who walk uprightly" (Ps. 84:11). God gives grace, which saves us. He gives glory, which we can return to Him. And He gives us good things, providing for our every need. What more could any woman need?

**9.** "My help and glory are in God" (Ps. 62:7 MSG).

# Chapter 2

**1.** "Who is this King of glory? The LORD of hosts, He is the King of glory" (Ps. 24:10). Paul calls God "the Father of glory" in Ephesians 1:17. And James refers to his own big brother "Our LORD Jesus Christ, the LORD of glory" (James 2:1).

**2.** "Not unto us, O LORD, not unto us, But to Your name give glory, Because of Your mercy, Because of Your truth" (Ps. 115:1). Though the thought of slipping into the center of attention may be an alluring one, the psalmist helps us to regain perspective. It's not about us. It's all about God. We can accept anything from His hand, so long as we know it will bring God greater glory.

**3.** "I am the LORD, that is My name; And My glory I will not give to another, Nor My praise to carved images" (Is. 42:8). God is perfect and holy. The idols men made were useless, and served only to reveal the rebelliousness in their hearts.

**4.** "You are worthy, O LORD, To receive glory and honor and power; For You created all things, And by Your will they exist and were created" (Rev. 4:11). When you start listing God's great works, you might as well begin at the beginning. Only God can claim the credit for bringing us into existence. That alone should garner our devotion.

**5.** "Saying with a loud voice: 'Worthy is the Lamb who was slain to receive power and riches and wisdom, And strength and honor and glory and blessing!'" (Rev. 5:12). Jesus made the ultimate sacrifice for our sake, and in the end, we will all have a chance to thank Him. He will receive the glory He is worthy to receive. In this verse alone, Jesus is declared worthy of power, riches, wisdom, strength, honor, glory, and blessing.

**6.** "The heavens declare His righteousness, And all the peoples see His glory" (Ps. 97:6). Creation wonderfully displays God's power and creativity and attention to detail. Its excellence—its very existence—brings Him glory.

**7.** "Please, show me Your glory" (Ex. 33:18). Moses wanted to see God for Himself, and dared to ask it. God allowed Moses a fleeting glimpse, but even that was overwhelming to a mere man. God's glory is an awesome thing!

**8.** "LORD, I have loved the habitation of Your house, And the place where Your glory dwells (Ps. 26:8). David's heart responds to the LORD, and he loves to spend time in the nearness of God: "So I have looked for You in the sanctuary, To see Your power and Your glory" (Ps. 63:2). When the people wished to be reminded of God's faithfulness and encouraged in their faith, they had only to look towards the sanctuary. There, the glory of God Himself rested.

**9.** "When all the children of Israel saw how the fire came down, and the glory of the LORD on the temple, they bowed their faces to the ground on the pavement, and worshiped and praised the LORD, saying: "For He is good, For His mercy endures forever" (2 Chr. 7:3). God is worthy of all glory. Someday we will all have the chance to bow down before Him. Then we can worship and praise Him in person. Until then, we content ourselves by giving Him glory now, and by holding fast to our belief that God is always good.

**10.** "For the earth will be filled With the knowledge of the glory of the LORD, As the waters cover the sea" (Hab. 2:14). God's glory will not be ignored. Someday, it will fill the earth so everyone will know it. It will blanket the earth like water.

# Chapter 3

**1.** "Bring to me all the people who are mine, whom I made for my glory, whom I formed and made" (Is. 43:7 NCV). Aha! Eureka! We've got it! People were made for God's glory. Our purpose here on earth is to bring glory to God.

**2.** "The heavens tell the glory of God, and the skies announce what his hands have made" (Ps. 19:1 NCV). The stars we admire so much in the night skies bring glory to God. Not to mention the planets, the comets, the falling stars, the bands of the Milky Way, distant galaxies, and the dancing aurora borealis.

**3.** "And every creature which is in heaven and on the earth and under the earth and such as are in the sea, and all that are in them, I heard saying: 'Blessing and honor and glory and power Be to Him who sits on the throne, And to the Lamb, forever and ever!'" (Rev. 5:13). Every created being—those in heaven, those on earth, even the creatures God has made will bring glory to God.

**4.** We are not fulfilling our original purpose. Something went very wrong! "For all have sinned and fall short of the glory of God" (Rom. 3:23). Sin has diverted us from our original purpose. And as a result, we fall short of glory.

**5.** "You who fear the LORD, praise Him! All you descendants of Jacob, glorify Him, And fear Him, all you offspring of Israel!" (Ps. 22:23). God started with Abraham and his descendents. Through them He planned to reach out to all the world. "All nations whom You have made Shall come and worship before You, O LORD, And shall glorify Your name" (Ps. 86:9). The day will come when every nation will give glory to God's name: "That every tongue should confess that Jesus Christ is LORD, to the glory of God the Father" (Phil. 2:11). At the very end, there will be no one holding out. Every single knee will bow and every single tongue will confess—all to the glory of God.

**6.** "But we all, with unveiled face, beholding as in a mirror the glory of the LORD, are being transformed into the same image from glory to glory, just as by the Spirit of the LORD" (2 Cor. 3:18). When we were saved, we were finally able to give God glory as we should. But God didn't stop there. Day by day, bit by bit, God is transforming us into His own image. The Spirit is working in our hearts and lives to bring this about. And as we are changed "from glory to glory," God receives all the more glory because of the excellence of His work.

**7.** "For you were bought at a price; therefore glorify God in your body and in your spirit, which are God's" (1 Cor. 6:20). When God arranged for our salvation, it was at great cost to Himself. Paul compares our redemption to God's purchasing our lives by sacrificing Jesus in our place. So bought, we owe God everything. Our lives should now be lived with God's glory as our highest priority.

**8.** "Call upon Me in the day of trouble; I will deliver you, and you shall glorify Me." (Ps. 50:15). God has saved us, and we glorify Him for that. God continues to transform our lives, and we bring Him glory for that as well. In this verse, we find God listens to us and answers our prayers. When He acts on our behalf, responding to our call, we have yet another reason to glorify God. And you can turn that around too. One of the reasons God does answer prayers is so the world will see His glorious working in the lives of those who belong to Him. So share those praises! Answered prayers are opportunities to return glory to God.

**9.** "Now to Him who is able to keep you from stumbling, And to present you faultless before the presence of His glory with exceeding joy, To God our Savior, Who alone is wise, Be glory and majesty, Dominion and power, Both now and forever.

Amen" (Jude 1:24, 25). God keeps us from stumbling, and He will present us fault-less someday. Because of this, Jude ascribes glory and majesty, dominion and power to God.

# Chapter 4

**1.** "Therefore glorify the LORD in the dawning light, The name of the LORD God of Israel in the coastlands of the sea" (Is. 24:15). First thing in the morning is always a good time to start glorifying God. When you wake up, start the habit of turning your thoughts to Him.

**2.** "Awake, my glory! Awake, lute and harp! I will awaken the dawn. I will praise You, O LORD, among the peoples; I will sing to You among the nations. For Your mercy reaches unto the heavens, And Your truth unto the clouds. Be exalted, O God, above the heavens; Let Your glory be above all the earth" (Ps. 57:8–11). David is up before the sun, and the strumming of his harp greets the first light of the morning sun. Many women rise extra early in order to spend a precious half–hour or so with the LORD before the rest of the household stirs.

**3.** "They also who dwell in the farthest parts are afraid of Your signs; You make the outgoings of the morning and evening rejoice" (Ps. 65:8). Thoughts of God can be bookends for your day. Touching base with Him mornings and evenings will give you reasons for rejoicing.

**4.** "When I remember You on my bed, I meditate on You in the night watches" (Ps. 63:6). "I stay awake all night so I can think about your promises" (Ps. 119:148 NCV). Often we wake in the night. These moments of nocturnal alertness can become opportunities to pray and to praise.

**5.** "In God we boast all day long, and praise Your name forever" (Ps. 44:8). "In Your name they rejoice all day long, and in Your righteousness they are exalted" (Ps. 89:16). You guessed it! We can give glory to God all day.

**6.** "But as for me, I will always proclaim what God has done; I will sing praises to the God of Israel" (Ps. 75:9 NLT). We will bring glory to God our whole life.

**7.** "Now to our God and Father be glory forever and ever. Amen" (Phil. 4:20). We will never exhaust our opportunities to give God all the glory. We will have eternity.

**8.** "For the Scripture says to Pharaoh, 'For this very purpose I have raised you up, that I may show My power in you, and that My name may be declared in all the earth'"

(Rom. 9:17). Even unbelievers find their way into God's plans and play their part in bringing glory to God. It's a comfort to remember, even when we flub up, God is able to pick up the pieces and use them for our good and His glory.

**9.** Sure, we can turn our thoughts towards God at any odd time throughout the day, but a wise woman will set aside regular times for meditation, prayer, and worship. We're each different, and there's no right time of day, but make the effort to set your appointment with God each day, and then keep it!

# Chapter 5

**1.** "I will make Your name to be remembered in all generations; Therefore the people shall praise You forever and ever" (Ps. 45:17). Now that's doing things on a grand scale! What's more, David accomplished that goal, for it was one God had placed in his heart. David glorified the LORD by accomplishing God's purposes for his life.

**2.** "Don't forget the things you have seen. Don't forget them as long as you live, but teach them to your children and grandchildren" (Deut. 4:9 NCV). Our children and grandchildren, and our friends' children and grandchildren, can have their lives changed by God if we show them the way and introduce them to the Savior.

**3.** "You love him even though you have never seen him. Though you do not see him, you trust him; and even now you are happy with a glorious, inexpressible joy. Your reward for trusting him will be the salvation of your souls" (1 Pet. 1:8, 9 NLT). Do you realize the simple fact that you love Jesus brings glory to God?

**4.** "He asked life from You, and You gave it to him—Length of days forever and ever. His glory is great in Your salvation; Honor and majesty You have placed upon him. For You have made him most blessed forever; You have made him exceedingly glad with Your presence" (Ps. 21:4–6). Our salvation brings glory to God. We are living proof that Jesus has conquered sin and death. Our eternal life with our LORD will be a constant testimony to God's greatness. We bring glory to God just by having faith!

**5.** "He who is faithful in what is least is faithful also in much; and he who is unjust in what is least is unjust also in much" (Luke 16:10). Maybe there is "much" in our future. But the future is in God's hands, and we are responsible right now for the "little" that has been given to us. If we are not faithful with the little, we will never be given responsibility for much.

**6.** "The name of our LORD Jesus Christ may be glorified in you, and you in Him, according to the grace of our God and the LORD Jesus Christ" (2 Thess. 1:12). No matter where you may go or what you may do, because you are a Christian, Jesus can be glorified in your life. What's more, you are glorified in Him. In a way, you benefit from His reputation, but then people also draw conclusions about Jesus based on your reputation. How 'bout them apples!

**7.** "Let your light so shine before men, that they may see your good works and glorify your Father in heaven" (Matt. 5:16). Live in such a way that you stand out from the crowd like a light in the darkness. Others will be drawn to you, be curious about you, and ask you why you are so different. Then you'll be able to tell them about Jesus.

**8.** "Eternal life to those who by patient continuance in doing good seek for glory, honor, and immortality" (Rom. 2:7). He states further how those who choose to follow a self–seeking path will suffer wrath and indignation from God. So stick to the Savior, sisters! His way may not be easy, but it is by far the best.

**9.** "If anyone speaks, let him speak as the oracles of God. If anyone ministers, let him do it as with the ability which God supplies, that in all things God may be glorified through Jesus Christ, to whom belong the glory and the dominion forever and ever. Amen" (1 Pet. 4:11). In other words, use the gift God gave you. Do the job in front of you. And do it all "to the glory of God" (1 Cor. 10:31). Living this way will glorify God.

# Chapter 6

**1.** "Jesus said to him, 'I am the way, the truth, and the life. No one comes to the Father except through Me'" (John 14:6). We cannot glorify God if we do not first come to Him, and there is only one right way—through Jesus.

**2.** "As His divine power has given to us all things that pertain to life and godliness, through the knowledge of Him who called us by glory and virtue" (2 Pet. 1:3). God has given us everything we need to live for His glory. Trust Him for the strength, the guidance, the encouragement, and the inspiration life requires of us.

**3.** "You shall love the LORD your God with all your heart, with all your soul, with all your mind, and with all your strength.' This is the first commandment" (Mark 12:30). Jesus reminds us we are to give God our love.

**4.** "Trust in the LORD with all your heart, and lean not on your own understanding" (Prov. 3:5). We can't always figure everything out, but we can put our trust in God. He will see us through.

**5.** "Give me understanding, and I shall keep Your law; Indeed, I shall observe it with my whole heart" (Ps. 119:34). "The proud have forged a lie against me, But I will keep Your precepts with my whole heart" (Ps. 119:69). "And it shall be that if you earnestly obey My commandments which I command you today, to love the LORD your God and serve Him with all your heart and with all your soul" (Deut. 11:13). The common thread is obedience. God asks us to obey Him wholeheartedly.

**6.** In these verses, David entreats the LORD with his whole heart and cries out to God. In other words, he prays with his whole heart. He prays, and the LORD hears.

**7.** "Praise the LORD! I will praise the LORD with my whole heart" (Ps. 111:1). Wholehearted praise is called for!

**8.** "Do not turn aside from following the LORD, but serve the LORD with all your heart… Only fear the LORD, and serve Him in truth with all your heart; for consider what great things He has done for you" (1 Sam. 12:20, 24). We are also asked to serve God.

**9.** "Seek the LORD your God, and you will find Him if you seek Him with all your heart and with all your soul" (Deut 4:29). We can be sure to find the LORD if we seek Him with all our hearts. God tells us for Himself how those who search for Him will find Him. And the one who seeks the LORD is called blessed and happy.

# Chapter 7

**1.** "Therefore, when you do a charitable deed, do not sound a trumpet before you as the hypocrites do in the synagogues and in the streets, that they may have glory from men. Assuredly, I say to you, they have their reward" (Matt. 6:2). Even a good thing loses its value when it's done for the wrong reason.

**2.** "All flesh is as grass, and all the glory of man as the flower of the grass. The grass withers, and its flower falls away" (1 Pet. 1:24). No matter how much we try to hold onto glory, we'll find it fades quickly. Glory isn't meant for us to keep, but to return to God.

**3.** "Thus says the LORD: 'Let not the wise man glory in his wisdom, Let not the mighty man glory in his might, Nor let the rich man glory in his riches; But let him who glories glory in this, That he understands and knows Me, That I am the LORD, exercising lovingkindness, judgment, and righteousness in the earth. For in these I delight,' says the LORD" (Jer. 9:23, 24). The only source of glory we have is in knowing God and understanding Him better.

**4.** "Therefore I have reason to glory in Christ Jesus in the things which pertain to God" (Rom. 15:17). Paul's reason for glorying came from two sources. He was able to glory in Jesus—the One who had grabbed his attention on the road to Damascus and saved him from himself. And, Paul gloried in the things pertaining to God. Just stop and think for a moment of all the things we can rejoice over and glory in: God's love for us, His plans for us, His grace, His gifts, His forgiveness, His patience—we could go on and on!

**5.** "He who speaks from himself seeks his own glory; but He who seeks the glory of the One who sent Him is true, and no unrighteousness is in Him" (John 7:18). Some people go through life trying to gain glory for themselves. This is what the Pharisees accused Jesus of. But Jesus declares He seeks only to glorify God. When we keep that as our goal in life, we follow in Jesus' footsteps.

**6.** "Do not let your adornment be merely outward—arranging the hair, wearing gold, or putting on fine apparel—rather, let it be the hidden person of the heart, with the incorruptible beauty of a gentle and quiet spirit, which is very precious in the sight of God" (1 Pet. 3:3, 4). God doesn't look on the outside of folks. He looks at the heart (1 Sam. 16:7), and it is the hidden person He evaluates. God's taste runs to quiet and gentle spirits. A woman adorned with this is precious in His sight.

**7.** "The righteous shall be glad in the LORD, and trust in Him. And all the upright in heart shall glory" (Ps. 64:10). The person who glories in the LORD is described as being righteous, upright in heart, and trusting of God. These qualities are hardly glamorous by the world's standards, but acceptable to God.

**8.** "Charm is deceitful and beauty is passing. But a woman who fears the LORD, she shall be praised" (Prov. 31:30). There will always be people who value a pretty face above all else, but there will also be those who know better than to judge by appearances. The fear of the LORD is lovelier than any outer beauty.

**9.** "Do not lay up for yourselves treasures on earth, where moth and rust destroy and where thieves break in and steal; but lay up for yourselves treasures in heaven, where neither moth nor rust destroys and where thieves do not break in and steal" (Matt. 6:19, 20). The message is clear—glory in God, and in the things that pertain to God. When we are distracted from this purpose by passing things, like wealth and beauty, we are investing our time and energy in things that will be taken away from us. Jesus says we need to store up treasures, but those treasures need to be heavenly ones, not earthly ones.

**10.** "But 'he who glories, let him glory in the LORD.' For not he who commends himself is approved, but whom the LORD commends" (2 Cor. 10:17, 18). Glory belongs to God. We should only glory in God. If that is our credo in life, the LORD Himself will commend us.

# Chapter 8

**1.** "I will offer sacrifices of joy in His tabernacle; I will sing, yes, I will sing praises to the LORD" (Ps. 27:6). David wanted to thank God for saving him from the enemy. It's like that chorus, "We bring the sacrifice of praise into the house of the LORD..." Nowadays we don't need sacrifices, but our sacrifice of joy is the song we raise up in praise and thanksgiving of the God who has saved us.

**2.** "Let the saints be joyful in glory; Let them sing aloud on their beds" (Ps. 149:5). Some songs arise from a heart filled with gratitude, like David's psalm in the previous question. But other songs are inspired by a joy that cannot be contained. In *The Message*, this same verse is translated, "Let true lovers break out in praise, sing out from wherever they're sitting."

**3.** "That you may with one mind and one mouth glorify the God and Father of our LORD Jesus Christ" (Rom. 15:6). Christians bring praise to God with one mind and with one voice. This does imply a focus on the message of our song—are you paying attention to the words crossing your lips? Paul also encouraged the unity that comes in corporate worship, because we are all supposed to be one in the Church.

**4.** "Rejoice in the LORD, O you righteous! For praise from the upright is beautiful. Praise the LORD with the harp; Make melody to Him with an instrument of ten strings. Sing to Him a new song; Play skillfully with a shout of joy" (Ps. 33:1–3). In this passage, both voices and instruments are mentioned. The psalmist describes singing a new song to the LORD, which implies finding new and creative ways to glorify God. The musicians are said to play skillfully, which implies excellence and giving our best to God. The songs are sung with joy, and the resulting music is described as beautiful. Praise is beautiful to God.

**5.** "You are holy, Enthroned on the praises of Israel" (Ps. 22:3). I love this verse! When we sing, when we worship, when we glorify God, He is there with us, enthroned on the praises.

**6.** "They shall sing of the ways of the LORD, For great is the glory of the LORD" (Ps. 138:5). We sing about the ways of the LORD—who He is and what He has done. If that is our topic in worship, it will truly be glorious, for great is the glory of the LORD.

**7.** "Give unto the LORD, O you mighty ones, Give unto the LORD glory and strength. Give unto the LORD the glory due to His name; Worship the LORD in the beauty of holiness" (Ps. 29:1, 2). Give to the LORD glory—glory that is His due.

**8.** "Ascribe greatness to our God" (Deut. 32:3). "I will ascribe righteousness to my Maker" (Job 36:3). "Ascribe strength to God" (Ps. 68:34).

**9.** "Then I will praise you with music on the harp, because you are faithful to your promises, O God. I will sing for you with a lyre, O Holy One of Israel. I will shout for joy and sing your praises, for you have redeemed me. I will tell about your righteous deeds all day long" (Ps. 71:22–24 NLT). The psalmist praises God because He is faithful in keeping His Promises and because He has redeemed him. These two things not only inspire song, but the desire to tell others about God's righteous deeds.

# Chapter 9

**1.** "You shall love the LORD your God with all your heart, with all your soul, and with all your strength. And these words which I command you today shall be in your heart. You shall teach them diligently to your children, and shall talk of them when you sit in your house, when you walk by the way, when you lie down, and when you rise up. You shall bind them as a sign on your hand, and they shall be as frontlets between your eyes. You shall write them on the doorposts of your house and on your gates" (Deut. 6:5–9). Here, God calls not only for wholehearted devotion, but a commitment to make the LORD a part of everyday life. His Word is to be in our hearts (memorized), and we should talk about them with our families. God and His Words should be on our lips while we're walking (or driving) along the way, while we're resting at home, when it's time for bed, at the start of every day. Keep God as near to you as your own hand, and keep His Word before your eyes. Write it on your walls if you have to!

**2.** "This sickness is not unto death, but for the glory of God, that the Son of God may be glorified through it" (John 11:4). Sickness can glorify God. "If you are reproached for the name of Christ, blessed are you, for the Spirit of glory and of God rests upon you. On their part He is blasphemed, but on your part He is glorified" (1 Pet. 4:14). Being insulted and coming under reproach can bring God glory. "This He spoke, signifying by what death he would glorify God" (John 21:19). God can be glorified in the death of those who belong to Him.

**3.** "For our light affliction, which is for but a moment, is working for us a far more exceeding and eternal weight of glory" (2 Cor. 4:17). No matter how difficult our life may seem, in the end we will call it a light affliction. In the face of eternity, the suffering will have been fleeting, momentary. And then, we will understand how God worked through those hardships for good, bringing glory to His name through them.

**4.** "Come and hear, all you who fear God, And I will declare what He has done for my soul" (Ps. 66:16). Your testimony—telling people how God is working in your life—brings glory to God.

**5.** "They shall speak of the glory of Your kingdom, And talk of Your power" (Ps. 145:11). Talk about what God has been doing in your heart. Let people know about God's plan of redemption and the power by which He carried it out. Tell others about His promises and how He has kept them.

**6.** "Being filled with the fruits of righteousness which are by Jesus Christ, to the glory and praise of God" (Phil. 1:11). When we are walking steadily with the Savior, He helps us to change and to grow. This is most evident in the spiritual fruit we bear. Lives characterized by love, joy, peace, patience, kindness, goodness, faithfulness, and self–control bring glory to God.

**7.** "He never doubted that God would keep his promise, and he never stopped believing. He grew stronger in his faith and gave praise to God" (Rom. 4:20 NCV). Abraham's unshakeable believe in God's ability to keep His Word brought glory to God's name. Abraham's faith was strengthened, and he made known the fact that God was responsible for all the blessings he enjoyed.

**8.** "For all things are for your sakes, that grace, having spread through the many, may cause thanksgiving to abound to the glory of God" (2 Cor. 4:15). Grace will cause thanksgiving to abound—thanksgiving for Jesus and salvation and eternal life. And this attitude of thankfulness, in spite of the persecution surrounding us, will bring glory to God.

**9.** "Finally, brethren, pray for us, that the word of the LORD may run swiftly and be glorified, just as it is with you" (2 Thess. 3:1). Paul asks believers to pray for the evangelization that is continuing through Paul's missionary journeys. It's his hope that God's Word will be glorified—proven true by the lives it continues to transform.

**10.** "If anyone speaks, let him speak as the oracles of God. If anyone ministers, let him do it as with the ability which God supplies, that in all things God may be glorified through Jesus Christ, to whom belong the glory and the dominion forever and ever. Amen" (1 Pet. 4:11). Use the gifts and abilities God has supplied. Speak the words God has given you to say. Reach out to one another as Jesus would have ministered. A life such as this will bring glory to God.

# Chapter 10

**1.** "My God shall supply all your needs according to His riches in glory by Christ Jesus" (Phil. 4:19). God will provide everything you need. In Acts 17:11, the Bereans were known as being fair–minded people. They received God's Word with readiness and searched the Scriptures every day to make sure the preaching they heard was in line with God's Word. "For Your name's sake, Lead me and guide me" (Ps. 31:3). God will lead us along for His glory. Peter says that God, through His divine power, has given us everything we need for life and godliness. "But as for me, my prayer is to You, O LORD, in the acceptable time; O God, in the multitude of Your mercy, Hear me in the truth of Your salvation" (Ps. 69:13). We pray, knowing God will answer in His time. And lastly, Deuteronomy says "the word is very near you, in your mouth and in your heart" (Deut. 30:14). Memorize the Scriptures, hiding them in your heart, and speak the Word, for there is power in it.

**2.** "Aspire to lead a quiet life, to mind your own business, and to work with your own hands, as we commanded you" (1 Thess. 4:11). Most of us are not asked to live out our faith on a grand scale. We're simply told to be obedient and faithful right where we are.

**3.** "That we may lead a quiet and peaceable life in all godliness and reverence" (1 Tim. 2:2). In this description, a quiet life is described with two characteristics: godliness and reverence. Godliness would be living in such a way as to reflect the character of God, trying to be like Jesus. Reverence would be having a proper fear and awe of God, leading to a life of respectful obedience.

**4.** "In quietness and confidence shall be your strength" (Is. 30:15). Ultimately, our source of strength is God. But we cannot be drawing strength from Him if we are ignoring Him. Quietness suggests a listening attitude, free from worry. And confidence is complete trust, knowing God is working for good no matter what happens. It is faith.

**5.** "Be still, and know that I am God" (Ps. 46:10). There are too many voices around us these days. If we want to follow God's leading, we must learn to be still and to recognize His voice. Recall when Elijah anticipated the voice of the LORD: "and after the earthquake a fire, but the LORD was not in the fire; and after the fire a still small voice" (1 Kin. 19:12). Even Elijah expected God to speak to him with a loud voice, like the earthquake and the fire. It was only when everything became still Elijah was able to hear His small voice. And when all things are quiet and we can focus on the promptings of God: "Your ears shall hear a word behind you, saying, 'This is the way, walk in it'" (Is. 30:21).

**6.** "O LORD, open my lips, And my mouth shall show forth Your praise. For You do not desire sacrifice, or else I would give it; You do not delight in burnt offering. The sacrifices of God are a broken spirit, A broken and a contrite heart—These, O God, You will not despise… Then You shall be pleased with the sacrifices of righteousness, With burnt offering and whole burnt offering; Then they shall offer bulls on Your altar" (Ps. 51:15–17, 19).

**7.** "For all the promises of God in Him are Yes; and in Him Amen, to the glory of God through us" (2 Cor. 1:20). God has kept His promises—every one of them. He will continue to do so, and every promise kept brings Him glory.

**8.** "Whatever you ask in My name, that I will do, that the Father may be glorified in the Son" (John 14:13). God is glorified when He answers our prayers.

# Chapter 11

**1.** "He who heeds the word wisely will find good, and whoever trusts in the LORD, happy is he" (Prov. 16:20). If you want to be wise in ordering your life, you must start with the Word of God. When you heed the Word (obey it) and trust the LORD, you will be blessed.

**2.** "We keep His commandments and do those things that are pleasing in His sight" (1 John 3:22). John says that followers of Christ are obedient and make an effort to do the things that please Him.

**3.** "If you love Me, keep My commandments" (John 14:15). You can't get much more straightforward than that! We say we love God. That's good! Let's live like we do!

**4.** "Do you not know that to whom you present yourselves slaves to obey, you are that one's slaves whom you obey, whether of sin leading to death, or of obedience leading to righteousness?" (Rom. 6:16). This Scripture calls us slaves. We are all servants, but we have a choice about whom we will serve. Will we serve sin, or God? If we obey our own selfish instincts, they will lead us to death. If we obey God, we will be righteous. It's one or the other. No neutral territory.

**5.** "Set your mind on things above, not on things on the earth" (Col. 3:2). We'll always struggle against sin and self—it's part of being human. But we can choose our goals. We can choose our path. We can decide what to think about and what rules our decisions. Paul says, "Choose God!" Set your mind on things above.

**6.** We know these passages. Matthew 5:3–12 is the Beatitudes. Galatians 5:22, 23 lists the fruits of the spirit. And Philippians 4:8 is that wonderful list Paul gives us of the kinds of things we should set our minds on. When these kinds of Scriptures are hidden in our hearts, they will lead us into right paths. They will help us to live to the glory of God.

**7.** d, a, g, h, f, c, e, b.

**8.** "If any of you lacks wisdom, let him ask of God, who gives to all liberally and without reproach, and it will be given to him" (James 1:5). Got wisdom? If not, James says God is happy to give it to us. Seek Him out through the pages of Scripture, and He will continue to add wisdom to you.

## Chapter 12

**1.** "Behold! My Servant whom I have chosen, My Beloved in whom My soul is well pleased!" (Matt. 12:18). God calls Jesus His Beloved, but He also designates Him a Servant—His own Servant. Jesus came to earth to do God's bidding: "The Son of Man did not come to be served, but to serve" (Mark 10:45). "I am among you as the

One who serves" (Luke 22:27). Jesus never wavered from His role. From beginning to end, He was humble and obedient to His Master.

**2.** "If anyone serves Me, let him follow Me; and where I am, there My servant will be also. If anyone serves Me, him My Father will honor" (John 12:26). If we want to serve Jesus, we are invited to follow His example. If we do so, we are promised we will join Him someday, and the Father will honor our efforts. It is worth the sacrifice.

**3.** "Present your bodies a living sacrifice, holy, acceptable to God, which is your reasonable service" (Rom. 12:1). Now that sounds like our old butler friend. He's given up his own rights and lives for the one he serves. That's his focus, his purpose. He has no other.

**4.** "You shall worship the Lord your God, and Him only shall you serve" (Matt. 4:10). We serve God. "You serve the Lord Christ" (Col. 3:24). We serve Jesus. "No one can serve two masters" (Matt. 6:24). We can't sit on the fence, trying to serve God while harboring our own agendas and ambitions. We must choose between serving God and serving our selfish motives.

**5.** In Acts 27:23, Paul says he belongs to God and he serves Him. In Romans 1:9, Paul says he serves God with his spirit.

**6.** "Though I am free from all men, I have made myself a servant to all, that I might win the more" (1 Cor. 9:19). In order to lead more men and women to Christ, Paul willingly put himself in the position of a servant.

**7.** The trustworthy servant is called "blessed" in Matthew 24:46. And when the Master finds his servant remaining faithful upon arrival, the commendation is great. "Well done, good and faithful servant; you were faithful over a few things, I will make you ruler over many things. Enter into the joy of your lord" (Matt. 25:21). No only does the faithful servant receive praise, she receives greater responsibility because she has proven herself worthy.

**8.** "I have glorified You on the earth. I have finished the work which You have given Me to do" (John 17:4). Amen!

# ✦ ACKNOWLEDGMENTS ✦

© Clairmont, Patsy, *The Best Devotions of Patsy Clairmont,* (Grand Rapids, MI: Zondervan Publishing House, 2001)

© Johnson, Barbara, *Daily Splashes of Joy,* (Nashville, TN: W Publishing Group, 2000)

© Johnson, Nicole, *Fresh–Brewed Life: A Stirring Invitation to Wake up Your Soul,* (Nashville, TN: Thomas Nelson, Inc., 2001)

© Johnson, Nicole, *Keeping a Princess Heart in a Not–So–Fairy–Tale World,* (Nashville, TN: W Publishing Group, 2003)

© Meberg, Marilyn, *The Best Devotions of Marilyn Meberg* (Grand Rapids, MI: Zondervan Publishing House, 2001)

© Swindoll, Luci, *I Married Adventure* (Nashville, TN: W Publishing Group, 2003)

© Walsh, Sheila, *The Best Devotions of Sheila Walsh and Unexpected Grace* (Grand Rapids, MI: Zondervan Publishing House, 2001)

© Wells, Thelma, *The Best Devotions of Thelma Wells* (Grand Rapids, MI: Zondervan Publishing House, 2001)

# ✦ STATEMENT OF FAITH ✦

*Women of Faith believes...*

The Bible to be the inspired, the only infallible, inerrant Word of God.

There is one God, eternally existent in three persons: Father, Son, and Holy Spirit.

He has revealed Himself in creation, history and Jesus Christ.

God's creation of the world and humankind with humanity's rebellion and subsequent depravity.

In the person and work of Jesus Christ, including His deity,

His virgin birth, His sinless life, His true humanity, His miracles,

His substitutionary death, His bodily resurrection,

His ascension to heaven, and His personal return in power and glory.

That for salvation of the lost, sinful man, regeneration by the Holy Spirit is absolutely essential.

Salvation is by grace through faith in Christ as one's Savior.

In the present ministry of the Holy Spirit by whose indwelling the Christian is enabled to live a godly life and to grow in the knowledge of God and Christian obedience.

In the resurrection of both the saved and the lost — the saved unto the resurrection of life and the lost unto the resurrection of damnation.

In the spiritual unity of believers in the LORD Jesus Christ and in the importance of church for worship, service and missions

# ✦ NOTES ✦

# ✦ NOTES ✦

# ✦ Notes ✦

# ✦ Notes ✦

# ✦ NOTES ✦

# ✦ NOTES ✦

# ✦ NOTES ✦

# ✦ NOTES ✦

# THE COMPLETE WOMEN OF FAITH®
## STUDY GUIDE SERIES

**WOMEN OF FAITH™**
STUDY GUIDE SERIES

To find these and other inspirational products visit your local Christian retailer.

www.thomasnelson.com

CPSIA information can be obtained at www.ICGtesting.com
Printed in the USA
LVOW12s1319040614

PP8507800001B/6/P

9 780785 251545